To Laura –
More garden
inspiration?
Much love, Ros
Diane + Ros
5/20/04

GARDENS OF THE
sun

TREVOR NOTTLE

Timber Press
Portland, Oregon

For my son,

James Edward Nottle

1975–1994

Designed by Kerry Klinner
Illustrations by Justin Sayers

First published in North America in 1996 by
Timber Press, Inc.
The Haseltine Building
133 S.W. Second Avenue, Suite 450
Portland, Oregon 97204, U.S.A.
1–800–327–5680 (U.S.A. and Canada only)

Reprinted 1997

Library of Congress Cataloging-in-Publication Data
Nottle, Trevor.
  Gardens of the sun / Trevor Nottle.
   p. cm.
  Includes bibliographical references (p.)
  ISBN 0–88192–365–6
  1. Gardening. 2. Mediterranean climate. 3. Landscape gardening.
  I. Title.
  SB454.3.M43N67 1996
  635––dc20   96–18760
                                                    CIP

Printed in Hong Kong

JACKET FRONT: *Succulents, cacti and all manner of drought-tolerant plants displayed at Le Jardin Exotique de Monte Carlo demonstrate the vast range of plants available to 'Mediterranean' gardeners.*

JACKET BACK: *Clipped evergreens at Jas Crèma, near Carpentras, Haute-Provence*

THIS PAGE: Allium sphaerocephalum

OPPOSITE PAGE: Lampranthus spectabilis, *ice plant*

contents

acknowledgments

This book owes a great deal to a band of dedicated gardeners from around the world; most have never met but all agreed to share their enthusiasms, frustrations, ideas and experiences to add to the store of knowledge and dreams which I had already accumulated from my own attempts at garden making in a townhouse garden, in a clifftop seaside garden and in a garden on the crest of a hill. All agree that gardening in a warm, dry climate where winters are wet and cool and summers hot and dry presents many challenges to creativity and to developing relaxing peaceful gardens in tune with their environment. Soils may be thin and impoverished, plant choices may be restricted by nature and by unadventurous nursery folk, but once old notions and myths about the nature of a 'good' garden are set aside and the whole business of garden making looked on as a journey of imagination and discovery, it is possible, indeed likely, that the problems will appear as fresh opportunities.

I acknowledge with sincere thanks the contribution made by the following gardeners:

June Adcock, Javea, Alicante, Spain

Jose Almandoz, San Sebastian, Spain

Jenny Andron, Molong, New South Wales

John Anstee, Arnside, Westmorland, England

Dianne Arthur, Hastings, New Zealand

Norma Ashley-Smith, Skiathos, Greece

Ros Auld, Borenore, New South Wales

Don Barrett, Millswood, South Australia

Olga Bezpalko, Socorro, New Mexico

Peter Bindon, Freemantle, Western Australia

Clive Blazey, Dromana, Victoria

Karen de Bont, Socorro, New Mexico

Fred Boutin, Tuolumne, California

Robyn Brader, Bowen Mountain, New South
    Wales

Mary Stella Brosius, Pasadena, California

Galen Burrell, Ridgefield, Washington

Anna Buxton, Edinburgh, Scotland

Jenny Bussey, Parcent, Alicante, Spain

John Calderwood, Lliber, Alicante, Spain

Pippy Cannon, Manildra, New South Wales

Mary Carpenter, Denia, Alicante, Spain

Dedie Carroll, San Mateo, California

Prudence Chandler, Skiathos, Greece

Bob Cheeseman, Menorca, Spain

Betsy Clebsch, La Honda, California

Rene Coffield, Creswick, Victoria

Harvey Collins, Millswood, South Australia

Tony Collinsplatt, Carpi, Italy

Spencer Compton, Santanyi, Mallorca, Spain

Graeme Cooke, Frankston, Victoria

Georgette Dixon, Stigler, Oklahoma

Cliff Douglas, Queen Creek, Arizona

Sharon van Enoo, Torrence, California

Gwen Fagan, Cape Town, South Africa

Brigitte Finlayson, Ruatoria, East Cape, New
    Zealand

Virginia Gardner, Santa Barbara, California

Tommy Garnett, Blackwood, Victoria

Don Gers, Santa Rosa, California

Heidi Gildemeister, Pollensa, Mallorca, Spain

Ken Gillanders, Longley, Tasmania

David Glenn, Ascot, Victoria

Moraig Godfrey, Grenfell, New South Wales

Bill Grant, Aptos, California

John Greenlee, Pomona, California

Sarah Guest, Melbourne, Victoria

Caroline Habouri, Kifissia, Greece

Harland J Hand, El Cerrito, California

Valmai Hankel, Adelaide, South Australia

Rita Harcourt, Skiathos, Greece

Tessa Hill, Albufeira, Portugal

Gordon Hughes, Paphos, Cyprus

Craig Irving, Euroa, Victoria

Noor Jackson, Ibiza, Ballearics, Spain

Alice Jeffery, Kew, Victoria

Anne Jenner, Crawley, Sussex

Esmond Jones, Muscle Creek, New South Wales

Danni Kaines, Balhannah, South Australia

Ms Keizer, Socorro, New Mexico

Felicity Kent, Mt Barker, South Australia

Barbara and Peter Knox-Shaw, Elgin, South
    Africa

Ms Kraft, Socorro, New Mexico

Wendy Langton, Torrens Park, South Australia

Belinda Legge, Kilcot, Gloucestershire

Kleine Lettunich, Watsonville, California

Dan Lloyd, Kew, London, England

Tony Mallia, Qormi, Malta

Panayotis Marselos, Athens, Greece

Clair Martin, San Marino, California

Ann Manning, Puerto Pollensa, Mallorca,
    Spain

Odile Masquelier, Lyon, France

Lew Matthews, Banks Peninsula, New Zealand

Jill Maunsell, Masterton, New Zealand

Dianne Maynard, Socorro, New Mexico

Gretl Meier, Stanford, California

Jane Miller, Granada, Spain

Jocelyn Mitchell, Beaufort, Victoria

Matthew Moores, Stirling, South Australia

Brian Morley, Gumeracha, South Australia

Dame Elisabeth Murdoch, Cranborne, Victoria

Phil and Marty Nesty, Concord, California

Howard Nicholson, Bundanoon, New South
    Wales

Tim North, Bowral, New South Wales

Lyn O'Brien, Pyree, New South Wales

Limonium
perezii, *sea
lavender*

Elizabeth Ronyn, Skiathos, Greece
Scilla Rosenberg, Kenthurst, New South Wales
Sharon Rowles, Bowen Island, British
    Columbia
Phillida Russell, Hastings, New Zealand
Karen Saxby, Adelaide, South Australia
Samantha Shaw, Brighton, England
Nevin Smith, Watsonville, California
Betty Spillmann, Canohes, France
Shirley Stackhouse, Killara, New South Wales
Jane Sterndale-Bennett, Andover, England
Joyce Stewart, Carmel Valley, California
Kaye Stokes, Greensborough, Victoria
Jacqui Sutherland, Featherston, New Zealand
Mike Tallman, Santa Rosa, California
Gil Teague, Balmain, New South Wales
Joan Tesei, Tor San Marino, Italy
Mike Treloar, Adelaide, South Australia
Sophie and Coralie Thomson, Summertown,
    South Australia
Derek Toms, Korbi, Attiki, Greece
Helen Vellacott, Castlemaine, Victoria
Sally Walker, Horsted Keynes, W. Sussex
Anne Marie Wall, Newport, Rhode Island
Francis Walling, Maslins Beach, South
    Australia
Daniel Walters, Crafers, South Australia
Iain Wheldon. Skiathos, Greece
Miriam Wilkins, El Cerrito, California
Anne Williams, Glendale, California
Brian Wills, Anduze, France
Daphne Wilson, Gore Bay, New Zealand
Barbara Worl, Berkeley, California

Peter Ormond, Hawkes Bay, New Zealand
Judith Phillips, Veguita, New Mexico
Roger Phillips, London, England
Helene Pizzi, Rome, Italy
Elizabeth Powdrell, Wairoa, New Zealand
Rosemary Poulton, Takapau, New Zealand
Pam Puryear, Navasota, Texas
Oscar Quitak, Ibiza, Ballearics, Spain

Photo credits:
Heather Angel: jacket front and back, pages 10, 14, 15, 24, 40, 60, 100, 114, 126, 163, 174
Roger Phillips: page 122
Alex Ramsay, Country Life Picture Library: page 64
Barbara Worl: page 32
Other photos by Trevor Nottle

introduction

It is a lovely day and I am ready to begin; my desk is well ordered with pens, pencils and markers in neatly arrayed pots, a large box of writing paper is at hand, the word processor and keyboard are set up and ready for my use. All around on shelves, stacked on table top and on the floor are books and journals, files of letters and newspaper clippings, notebooks, scrapbooks, catalogues, seed lists, sketches and photographs.

This will be a fine book; it is already well known to me and I like it; it has been in my life for four years and more, and now I am writing it.

My ideas begin to stir and move more quickly as I make a start on getting the words down. What is it I want to tell you? It is that gardening in a warm, dry climate can be exhilarating, exciting, restful, serene and above all enjoyable. But there is another idea that seems to be more elusive, an idea that's secret in the way it hides from us the contentment that we seek in making a garden. It is simple enough, but how we are so easily tricked. Let me tell you about it so we may all understand things better. It is a lovely midsummer day. There have been steady showers on and off for three days and each morning finds the garden enfolded in mist. The garden is heavy with rain, weighed down with sodden leaves, dripping big drops of cold, cold water. Clouds hang low and the mists sweep over the crest of the hills and envelop the garden. A small thought diverts me from my task, 'Weren't those Tibetan poppies lovely? What a beautiful luminous blue. Perhaps I could get just two or three? They would look great in that shady spot under the bedroom window and this weather would surely see them well settled and feeling at home?' Before my dreaming eyes a garden builds, filled with all the glories of an English flower garden. I add Sissinghurst to Hidcote, pile on top Great Dixter, Barnsley, Cranbourne, Hatfield and Highgrove. With thoughts racing, further horticultural trophies are gathered in: Giverny, Les Moutiers, Titoki Point, La Mulatiere and Ashland Hollow. I pick the eyes out of the past, taking what I wish — from Hammersmith Farm I choose a lush water garden; misty borders and Oriental walls from The Eyrie; the Classical ruins of Hagley reflected in mirrored pools; a garden of topiary spires from Sutton Courtney, and the opalescent gems of half a hundred others . . . until, under the weight of its own impossibility, the dream collapses.

How swayed we are, all of us, by glossy magazines, books, travellers' tales and television programs that stir our dreams and memories of other places; places that in our hearts are where we are persuaded we want to be or that we want to reproduce; places unlike our own warm, dry climates, where one would think we would feel comfortable and truly at home.

So what is this small secret idea, this key to contentment with our gardens and feeling a sense of belonging in our warm, dry climates? It is surely to know that we live where we live; that we are where we are; that we intend to stay and that, however much we dream, and despite whatever we may do, we cannot grow the likes of *Meconopsis betonicifolia* without inviting disappointment and frustration. Sissinghurst, Hidcote, Giverny and all the rest are lovely and right in their place, but are not this place, your place and my place — these warm, dry places. Knowing this, it is easier then to put dreams where they belong and set out to discover, see, understand and eventually know the sense of place that is the environment where you and I live. The rains that have fallen at midsummer are the very last rains. They will soon give way to the heat and drought of high summer; greenery and water will be precious, the resting landscape will

8

be yellowed, dry and dusty until dews and mists presage the arrival of the wet season and with it the plants and flowers which flourish with the rains. Like the garden, we too should rest during the season of heat and drought, storing energy and ideas against the arrival of the seasons for gardening.

Do not fret about giving up impossible dreams. They were never meant to be. Do not harbour anxieties about giving up established ideas and traditions transplanted from other places with different climates. They do not serve us well. Think instead of the fun of exploring the world for ideas that will work and plants that will thrive in your warm, dry garden. Charge your energy for shopping in nurseries and by mail-order catalogue. Be confident that we can learn much from each other and from those who have made gardens in climates similar to our own for hundreds of years. Gather ideas from Spain, Italy, Provence and colonial gardens of California. Observe La Mortola, Montagne du Luberon, Quinta de Bacalhoa, Buda and Boschendal. Success and satisfaction will grow out of a creativity that exists comfortably within the 'economy' of the local environment and draws on the lessons of the past to synthesise a new framework for garden making in those parts of the world where the climate is warm and dry. Dream then new dreams of creating gardens that make the most of the flowers of autumn, winter and spring; dream of a summer spent relaxed and cool in a subtle garden of deep shade made cool with varied greenery and enlivened with the gentle drip and plash of water. Dream of being at one with the place where you live, of working with the climate and developing a sense of place.

One Continuous
summer

'Where do you live?' and 'What do you grow?' are the two foremost questions whenever gardeners are newly met and for new gardeners the answers are rather a problem; if the reply meets with general approval from the surrounding bevy of horticulturists all will be well, but if the answer receives no comment or worse, brings forth a negative reaction, the newcomer may as well realise that they are forever condemned to the compost heap of gardening life

Would it not be smart then to know the right answers before entering upon any social event where gardens and gardening are likely to come up? Naturally the first answer will support the second, thus establishing your credibility and nous. Better not be too specific though, lest some crusty listener question you too closely about their nephew who just happens by chance to live down the road, on the next rise, in the nearby village or is married to the daughter of the Lord of the Manor. A good open-

Previous pages:

(p. 10)

Colourful and

hardy

succulents

transform a

difficult

situation in Le

Jardin

Exotique de

Monaco.

(p. 11) Scaevola

aemula *makes*

an attractive

ground cover.

ended reply to 'Where do you live?' would be 'At about 300 metres above sea level, facing south on a gentle slope with neutral soil and a rainfall of around 45 cm per year'. As you can see, this says a lot without giving anything away, and gives you something to build on for the second question. Now, without a doubt this whole business is to do with establishing who has the greatest horticultural clout, so you must understand that one-up-personship is the game to be played, and it must be played hard if you are to avoid being squelched by more experienced players. There are only three answers to the question 'What do you grow?' and they are *'Rhododendron sino-grande, Davidia involucrata* and *Tecophilaea cyanocrocus'*. A sighed confession of having no luck with *Ramonda myconii* and *Raoulia mammillaris* will establish at once that you know your onions, or in this case your difficult and desirable plants.

The purpose of such questioning settles not only whether or not you can be admitted to the company of 'real' gardeners, but also that you understand that there are such things as plants of such rarity, difficulty and down-right cussedness that every 'real' gardener aspires to grow them and hence knows also that there are certain locations for garden making that are pre-eminent. In Australia, the mecca of all respectable gardeners is the uppermost slopes of Mt Dandenong, in particular the village of Olinda in Victoria. It is here that all of the above inventory of plant jewels will feel at home and most likely prosper. Likewise there is the whole state of Oregon in the USA; it seems at least half of the gardeners I have met in the United States of America plan to move there because the climate is so perfect for growing all kinds of the 'best' plants. It seems typical that an entire state of America should be ideal gardening country, so great is the urge among gardeners there to collect and grow everything. In France, the *Hortus Paradisus* may well be between Dieppe and Vernon, while in England it could be in the vicinity of Chipping Camden; on the Iberian Peninsula it is possibly around Sintra, and in Italy it surely lies near Sermoneta — or is it just outside Tivoli?

But what of those of us who must garden in less-than-ideal places; for whom *Rhododendron sino-grande* is no less an impossibility than *Tecophilaea cyanocrocus?* How shall we counter the claims of this superior band of horticulturists who draw on the heritage of Farrer, Wilson, Forrest, Kingdon Ward among others? They contend that along with peaty, acidic soils, benign cool climates and thousands of litres of purest rainwater, that deciduous woodland gardens are a *sine qua non*.

My first tactic is to intone three alternatives to the trio *ne plus ultra* listed above. I rather like the sound of *Cantua buxifolia, Carpentaria californica* and *Euphorbia ingens* myself, but almost any combination of relative unknowns of the plant world will do so long as

1
2

they come from places where the climates are warm and dry. *Trichocereus spachianus* sounds pretty assertive and *Orbexilum pedunculatum* or *Ferocactus hamatacanthus* sound positively intimidating. Perhaps softly mouthing *Brahea moorei* or *Beschorneria septemptrionalis* will be enough to produce a stunned silence among the cool-climate *cognoscenti*.

Fouquieria splendens is probably going too far; it may even be thought by some to be offensive!

Now it may be that these plants are unknown to you. This is not, however, particularly important when conversing with cool-climate snobs. What you do need to know in the game of being one-up on the superior brand of persons who do grow *Rhododendron sino-grande et al.* is that most likely they will have no knowledge of these other plants, which are so far outside their realm of connoisseurship. Chinks such as this in the knowledge of elitist gardeners create a small silence which you can fill, as quickly as possible, with conversation about the wonderful gardens made in warm, dry climates and tell of the beautiful and strange plants that thrive in those conditions. Even without knowing the specifics of plant rarities and their discovery, it is possible to carry off a discussion on the basis of famous gardens such as the Jardin Exotique de Monaco, the gardens around the Huntington Library in Pasadena and the Cuesta Linda estate (now Lotusland) in Santa Barbara, those of La Mortola near Ventimiglia on the Italian Riviera or those at Ste Claire near Hyères on the French Riviera. All of these gardens were made in warm, dry climates by people who wanted to explore the possibilities of growing plants in associations and landscapes that were utterly different from the more usual woodland gardens that had grown out of the numerous plant introductions from China, Japan and the Himalayas, that required mild and cool conditions.

Even during the 1920s, when woodland gardens and cool-climate perennials were at the peak of their popularity, the very same gardeners who were using these plants and the garden style in England, the United States and France, were at the same time making gardens suited to warm, dry climates in California, the French and Italian Rivieras and on the Spanish Coast; some even gardened in exotic places such as Egypt, Kenya, Malta and Crete. The very best gardeners of the age were eagerly indulging themselves in an exciting diversity of gardening styles that called for owning gardens in different climatic zones. We may not enjoy such luxury as this today, but we who garden in warm, dry climates should not feel disadvantaged by our situation. We should look to the enthusiasms of great gardeners such as Lawrence Johnston (Hidcote Manor and Serre de la Madone), Ellen Willmott (Warley Place and Boccanegra) Vicomte

1
3

Charles de Noailles (Villa Noailles) and take heart from the beautiful gardens they made. A warm, dry climate need not be a restriction on horticultural excellence, garden style or to gardening pleasures.

While the stunning effect of such bold assertions may hold the cold-climate bores in check for a while, they are not so easily reduced to acceptance of other views so as to withdraw from discussion. It is wise therefore to gradually build up a store of evocative scenes which they will recognise as having equivalents which they understand. Instead of sheets of bluebells in a wood, refer to blankets of babiana; suggest that great drifts of freesias are even better than masses of snowdrops; praise the stunning displays of cantua, datura and plumbago that can only be had in areas like the Mediterranean; sing the flowery glories of yucca, eschscholtzia and ceanothus such as are seen in California, and revel in the architectural silhouette, striking foliage and flowers of *Aloe plicatilis*, *Agave parryi* and *Genista aetnensis*. Let it be known quietly that *Cyclamen africanum* and *Cyclamen rohlfsianum* grow outdoors under shrubs in places where the climate is warm and dry.

So just what is a warm, dry climate, or to use another common and equally general term 'a Mediterranean climate'? There are no doubt some fairly lengthy and scientific climatological and meteorological definitions and there will exist in some countries complex maps that link up monthly average rainfalls, minimum and maximum temperatures, degrees of frost, absence of frost, hours of daylight by means of hatching and shading and colours that pinpoint distinct climatic zones, but these can be as puzzling as they can be helpful, and many of us find that even when we understand such diagrams and definitions, our particular microclimate still manages to defy inclusion.

In a broad definition, those places that can be described as having a warm temperate climate are situated approximately between latitudes 30° and 40° north and south of the Equator. Average summer temperatures are about 21°C (70°F) and average winter temperatures are about 10°C (50°F). There is no real cold season when all plant

Fouquieria splendens, *the ocotillo in Arizona.*

growth ceases to be active. Summers are dry and hot, and the mild winter is the rainy season. The presence of mountain chains and ranges of high hills increases the rainfall, as in the case of the Sierra Nevada in California and the Mount Lofty Ranges in South Australia. Winters may also have frosty nights and even light snowfalls, but these generally are infrequent and rarely severe. Even the rainy winter typically has many periods of fine, sunny weather. The characteristic summer drought of a Mediterranean climate tends to last about three months, though this will be lengthened nearer Tropics and shortened towards the North and South Poles. The drought may sometimes be

Euphorbia ingens *makes a striking silhouette at Lotusland, California.*

1
5

slightly relieved by summer thunderstorms, especially in inland areas away from the moderating influence of the seas. It is worth noting that the Mediterranean climate occurs on the western margins of the great land masses. Apart from the Mediterranean basin, which stretches 3200 kilometres (2000 miles) west to east, the other warm, dry climatic zones of the world tend to be very narrow, generally confined between an ocean or sea to the west and a natural geographical barrier — mountains, hills or desert to the east. Such is the case in California, the Cape Province of South Africa, central Chile, Western Australia and South Australia.

Aside from these typical Mediterranean-type climates, there are many other areas where conditions and geography combine to produce similar, or at least somewhat similar, seasonal weather patterns. Although gardeners in these areas may not rightly claim to garden in a Mediterranean climate, they assert that the problems they face, particularly those that arise from summers that are hot and dry with a rainless period that extends over two months or more, are akin to those that confront gardeners in the defined zones. Thus they find themselves included in the pages of this book.

More interesting perhaps to gardeners than the strict, or even approximate, zones where the climate is warm and dry are the seasons which occur. It is our thinking about the seasons which so strongly colours our thoughts about what should be happening in a garden at a particular time of the year. Is it not true that most of us think familiarly of the traditional spring, summer, autumn and winter cycle associated with Anglo-European cultures? We speak of events in our lives, and in our gardens, in terms of this seasonal cycle. It is so ingrained in our culture that we refer to it automatically every day. It is a part of our language. This may seem obvious and natural; a perfectly ordinary thing that everyone knows. But how does it compare with what really happens in your climate? Scrutinised from this perspective, the traditional progress of the seasons may not line up in the way we would expect.

If it is necessary to refresh your memory banks, the traditional progress of the seasons is that of spring when things burst into growth from a dormant state and grow strongly as the days lengthen and the temperatures rise. Summer arrives with wildflowers and garden display reaching their height with the support of gentle and frequent showers of rain and warm, mild weather. As the plants mature and ripen, the day's length begins to shorten and the season progresses into autumn; day temperatures begin to decline, light rains continue but in time plants become dormant. The growing year ends with most plants being dormant, cold temperatures, frost and snow and short days darkened by cloud cover.

The progress of growth follows the same pattern, but in a Mediterranean climate the timing is very different. The growing period begins as the days begin to shorten and the temperatures to fall and coincide with the arrival of the first rains, in the old parlance this is called autumn, although it may be the season of mists it is clearly not the season of mellow fruitfulness. As the days become shorter and cooler, and the rains intensify, growth surges ahead in the lush conditions: this is winter, but most plants native to the region are far from dormant. As the days begin to lengthen and the temperatures to rise the rains continue and the plants swell their seeds and begin to mature, this period corresponds with spring despite the pattern of growth being more like that of autumn. Eventually, the

ABOVE:
Summer landscape at rest—dry grasses and trees
LEFT: Aloe bainesii, a lofty tree aloe

1

7

days become warm, long and sunny and the rains taper off until there is none and the seeds are ripe and may be dispersed, or held fast in drought-proof pods. Growth ceases and plants, evergreen and deciduous, are in a state of green stasis. This is plainly summer as we know it; beach weather and time for relaxing in the cool shade of trees; our bodies tell us that it is not the time to be working frenetically on garden chores. It is sensible to avoid the sun and environmentally sympathetic to have a garden that though it may be (mostly) green is also at rest.

Reviewing the patterns of weather and the progress of plant growth against the traditional seasons can be an important first step in getting into tune with the actual seasons that operate in your area. Once this is understood, it is not difficult to think out a new pattern of gardening that goes with the flow of the seasons rather than trying to impose a cycle that is alien to the natural conditions. Knowing when plants begin their growing period in nature can give a good lead to the best time to plant new plants; knowing when the rains are at their heaviest and most reliable can help to decide which plants, being then in full growth, can be chosen (to save on irrigation in the dry season); knowing how long the period of natural green dormancy may last can give guidance in developing gardening strategies to provide interest and colour without entailing onerous chores and untimely work.

Sometimes weather patterns and records will be available from meteorological offices, departments of agriculture or their local agents; these will help to develop that sensitivity to the local pattern of seasons, but it is as well to develop your own weather eye by observing and noting the winds, clouds, rain and heat; and when things grow, when they flower, when they seed and die. There may well be local weather lore and plant wisdom to be gathered from residents and neighbours — all can help to bring about that fine tuning and planning which makes or breaks the establishment of a garden. It is hard to credit the importance of keeping a garden notebook that from time to time includes weather observations, but intimate acquaintance with the weather in the immediate area can be very helpful.

In 1969, an English woman who had worked as a lecturer in urban design at Harvard University retired to a house she had bought for the purpose near Athens in Greece. Her name was Jacqueline Tyrwhitt and her aim was to make a garden at Sparoza that was Mediterranean in feel and in tune with the local environment. She kept many detailed notes, including the weather, as the work slowly went ahead over the next fifteen or so years and before her death in 1984 she had compiled an extensive manuscript of the plants she grew, her successes and failures, the conditions in the garden that guided her choice of plants and the patterns of weather that supported the cycle of seasons there. Without the observations and the notes, the progress of the garden would have been by happenstance and fortuitous accidents; as it was the garden grew by accumulated knowledge and wisdom. And it is a lovely garden that is now maintained by the Goulandris Natural History Museum under the curatorship of Sally Razelou. The notebooks will eventually be published by the museum and Jacqueline Tyrwhitt's rich store of experience will be available to readers everywhere. But even then it will be a good idea to keep records of your own patch.

Beside the pattern of seasons and the extremes of temperature, there are two other important aspects of climate that are not to be ignored by those who make gardens in warm, dry climates. The first is the amount of rainfall, and the rate of evaporation; and the second is wind.

As always, rainfall may be more or less according to local conditions, but in general the amount of rain that falls in an area with a Mediterranean climate is about 750 millimetres (30 inches) per year. Importantly for gardeners, this falls mostly in the coolest months and often there is none at all during the hottest months. What is not often realised is that worse than no rain falling is the very high rate of evaporation which may accompany the drought. With high daytime temperatures often over 27°C (80°F), and which during heatwaves may hover for weeks at over 38°C (100°F), the rate of evaporation can be equivalent to 1780 millimetres (70 inches) per year and more; more evaporation than in actual fact falls as rain! This means that the ground dries out very rapidly and that any plants in active stages of growth will be placed under extreme stress, possibly to the point of dehydration, collapse and complete desiccation. Surely a compelling reason for growing mainly plants that have a period of green dormancy during the hottest, driest months? And also a good argument for using as much mulch as possible to keep the soil cool and to conserve as much moisture in the soil as possible, equally applicable whether it is expensive tap water from town supplies or if it is precious stored rainwater from tanks and dams.

How the rain falls is important too. Does your area get torrential downpours that scour and wash away precious soil? Do you get sea mists or hill fogs at night? Does rainfall in your area build up slowly and taper off gradually throughout autumn, winter and spring (excuse my use of such terms) or do the rains begin and cease with a more marked intensity? How long does the wet season last? What about hail storms? Besides the damage they can wreak, they do deliver some useful quantities of water, but is it a reliable source of water for the garden or a chancy 'top-up' to the annual rainfall?

19

Having some idea about the pattern of rainfall, its intensity and duration over the year is very helpful in choosing plants for garden making in warm, dry areas for it enables us to choose plants which we know will have ceased active growth, or almost ceased active growth, by the time the rains begin to abate for the year. By choosing plants which complete their annual growth within the months of natural rainfall, the need for extensive summer irrigation can be greatly reduced or eliminated. By choosing to garden with plants that grow very little during the hottest and driest months, great savings can be made on water consumption and on the expenditure of personal energy — if you are smart in your choice of plants there will not be much to do but sit in the shade and relax while the most debilitatingly hot months pass.

Cantua pyrifolia, *a hardy shrub from Chile*

In some parts, bad winds are called *Mariah* — at least according to Rogers and Hammerstein — but where I live they are unimaginatively called 'northerlies' and they blow hot, strong and destructive for a few days almost every summer. At these times everyone keeps an eye on the hills and about the

skyline for the ominous, tight, billowing, dun-coloured clouds that tell of a bushfire.
The 'northerlies' have the capacity to generate feelings of prickliness on the skin and a
crackling dryness that makes breathing uncomfortable; the oven-like dry heat seems to
call out bad tempers, irritability and, it is said, madness. Those who have lived in places
where these winds blow can almost tell by the feel of the air on their skin that firebugs
and incendiaries will be out and about, stirred to action by the extreme weather. In
other parts there are equally worrisome summer winds that threaten mayhem in the
garden. The *Santa Ana* is a hot, summer wind that blows out of the inland deserts,

*A haven from
the heat and
harsh sunshine
of summer; a
rustic pergola
in Australia*

2
1

through the mountain passes and sears the coastal plains of southern California, while the Mediterranean shores of France and Italy can be scoured by the *Sirocco* and blasted by the *mistral*, and the *tramontana*. The *leveche* plagues gardeners in different parts of Spain. Those who garden in parts of Greece can be scourged by the *livas* and the *shilok*. The *khasmin* desiccates Malta, and Egypt gets the heat treatment from the *simoon*. Wherever they blow, the winds are hot and dry, and they rapidly scorch plants and parch the soil. Frequently the winds are extremely gusty, often persist for weeks and always create very discomforting conditions that somehow portend trouble; it is not surprising that these winds are described as maelstroms.

Protection from hot, dry winds is a major consideration for gardeners in Mediterranean climates. Plants need the protection of shadecloth and taller plants nearby and people need the protection, cool and shade of tall spreading trees or overhead canopies of canvas and latticework. While shelter from hot winds is physically important to plants and people, the psychological impact of such protection is at least equally important if we are to feel comfortable about living in warm, dry climates.

But can there be any protection from those elitist gardeners who demand to know where you live and what you grow? Their intention is to let you know that however good you may be at growing plants and however beautiful, satisfying and intimate your garden may be, it cannot stand a whit alongside those where *Rhododendron sino-grande*, *Davidia involucrata* and *Tecophilaea cyanocrocus* can be persuaded to grow. Obviously your education as a gardener cannot be complete if you do not strive to better yourself by achieving these much-sung glories. Bluntly put, this is a sort of horticultural bastardisation for no matter that you wanted to, and were able to grow these plants, acceptance would still be conditional. After all they could not possibly be grown as well as they are on Mt Rich and Lofty. This is not what gardening is about, this is a put-down; it is not a benign comment.

This seems rather a long way from the subject of climate despite the 'heat' of the discussion, and yet it is not so far as at first might seem for it is the climate of the area that we live in which dictates to a large degree what we can grow and what we will be seeking to create in our gardens. Our history may be European, our terminology (however confused) may speak of other weather patterns in cooler, wetter regions and our sentiments may attach certain plants to our thinking about gardens, but these frames of reference should never form the boundaries by which we define our gardening. However much water we may apply by hose and pipe and sprinkler and jet we cannot really turn our warm, dry climate into something different. Whatever cool-climate plants we may cosset, mollycoddle and pamper we cannot ever pretend that such like as *Meconopsis betonicifolia* will flourish as they do in the wilds of Tibet or in the gardens at Inverewe. Try as we might, the glories of the English perennial border will not shine forth in months of colour under a hot sun and a rainless sky. This Anglo-European garden history that we carry in our minds does not explain everything once and for all; it simply tries to provide a system that helps understanding. It is, however not the only system and there is nothing to prevent the evolution of new systems. This landscape that we carry in our hearts keeps us tied to an impossible dream; it cripples our creativity with discontent.

To break free of the feeling that there are better places to garden and better plants to grow, we have to see beyond the flowers and through the garden styles to understand that what drove the development of gardens, particularly in the 19th century, was exploration. And it is to exploration that we must turn again in order to come to new plants, new styles and new ideals. Along the way there will be dreams and whispers of things to build on from the past; there will be nightmares as we struggle with new visions of gardening and new techniques of cultivation, but there will be excitement and the thrill of going forward after a long period of gardening in retrospect. And this time we will create using plants that are suited to our warm, dry climates; styles will evolve that are in tune with the heat and dryness of summer; ideals will form that eschew pretence and artifice and accept that our gardens must be gardens of the sun.

ROCKS AND OTHER
hard places

SOILS AND SITES

'Perhaps you would like to get in touch with my daughter?' one correspondent writes from the rain-shadow dry east coast of New Zealand. 'She has two acres on Bowen Island near Vancouver, her garden is on a very rocky steep slope; very wet in winter as the heavy rains pour down the tree-clad cliffs and very, very dry through summer.'

The idea of British Columbia or New Zealand being 'dry' may seem incongruous, but there it is; where the seasons or settings combine heat and the want of water together there are challenges for imaginative, responsive gardeners to meet wherever they live. Another letter-writer from Italy describes his ground 'in a former scrapyard from which I have removed 500 square metres of oil-contaminated gravel.... I shall do desultory planting of shrubs and allow to grow on the ground what the ecology permits, removing what I don't like — a sort of controlled wilderness.'

PREVIOUS PAGES:

(p. 24) Clipped

evergreens at

Jas Créma,

near

Carpentras,

Haute-

Provence

provide a

suitably formal

setting for the

chateau

despite

difficult soil

conditions and

an exposed

site, and (p. 25)

a massive

terrace wall

that would

benefit from a

bold planting

scheme

(detail).

Rocks and hard places indeed, yet no greater a challenge than that faced by my New Zealand friend who gardens right on the shingle of the Pacific Ocean with an understratum of purest beach sand and the occasional boulder protruding, or worse still hidden just below the soil, commanding endless digging to discover if it can be moved or must be incorporated into the scheme of things.

My own experience has not been quite so trying as any of these; I do not quite get flooded, nor do I have the problems of residual industrial waste or those of randomly scattered boulders; neither is my soil perfect, but I am working on it steadily and achieving pleasing improvements in its condition and state of health.

Soil improvement is much talked about but most often in reference to achieving quick 'fixes' to conditions which may or may not abate with such treatment. A dose of iron chelates, a sprinkle of gypsum, a dusting with flowers of sulphur, a smattering of worm castings, a drenching soak of 'cow-pat tea' or a drizzle of pigeon poo – chemical and otherwise, all have their adherents. And all of them are 'right'! Their particular pet potion can alone alleviate problems with the soil. No kidding. Listen to them any day on talkback radio gardening programs.

How can we all be wrong (not following their pernickety dictates) and still have gardens that actually do manage to grow living, green plants? The commonsense answer is of course that we are not so wrong after all, but maybe our soils could be better looked after than they are and they could almost certainly be improved. How best to do that is a problem only to those who want to make it a problem. The happy-minded remainder can dig and delve among the theories and the dirt and develop a pattern of land care that experience shows give the best results and that best suits them.

In our own case, we found the site of our future garden to be a wasteland of antiquated, rusty irrigation equipment, barbed wire, derelict machinery, shards of household crockery and broken glass, and long-lost cap guns and other assorted toys. Underneath, the shallow topsoil had long ago been scraped clean away and sold as loam to some city gardener. Left behind was a thin veil of clay over a substratum of shale with occasional pockets of deeper topsoil remaining. Somehow, it managed to support an orchard of stumpy apple trees, a very large Ponderosa pine, two half-hearted hollies and an ancient pair of sunbronzed camellias. In winter the slope of the hillside and the want of soil combine to produce an almost constant flow of surface water for several months on end, while in summer the western exposure of the land sees the soil baked and dried of all its moisture within a month of the rains stopping. This may sound dismally familiar to some.

So what to do with it? Buy a truckload of someone else's backyard to make good the loss. No, too expensive and too great a risk of terrible weeds like bindweed (*Convolvulous arvensis*) and soursob (*Oxalis pes-caprae*). Get it tilled, dug and double dug? No, the work is too hard. Order truckloads of commercial compost? No, you rarely know what you are buying or what its properties may add to your already problematic soil. Hand the problem over to someone else and get it landscaped by a contractor? No, it is more satisfying to do it yourself.

Where to start then? The best way to get started on soil improvement is to get it cleared of any rubbish that previous owners may have blessed you with, and get it cleared of undergrowth and weeds, but leave any trees, shrubs or other plants that may be useful. In the months ahead, try to keep regrowth mown so that observations can be made to see what surprises may grow up once the dross is cut away. Almost anything can burst into growth that has lain semi-dormant for ages, especially in old derelict gardens where roses, bulbs and perennials may emerge with strong new growth.

At this stage it is really smart not to hurry things, so if plants held over for transplanting from previous gardens or gift plants have to be found a home, it is best to set up a holding bed where they can be set out awaiting transfer to their allocated places.

Make a plan of work that divides the garden up into manageable-sized plots that can be conveniently dealt with. Experience may dictate that these plots will be all manner of sizes and differently shaped, but no matter so long as they are large enough to be worked each in one burst and not so large that they demand the attendance of all family members to do the work. Planning ahead somewhat, usually a week or two is plenty of time, ensure that newspapers are hoarded and kept dry; scour the local newspapers and the community for sources of sawdust, buzzer shavings and chips, shredded leaves — freshly mulched will do well enough and any animal manures and vegetable litter from stables, stalls and coops. As a great deal of such materials will be needed, explore all possible avenues of supply, farming relatives, municipal cooperatives, local small industries. There was a time when much of these materials could be had free for the taking, but the times being less generous, nowadays these things often cost money. It is fateful to stint so keep on the lookout: buy what you must but do be happy to scrounge when opportunities arise for thrift. Mucking out the stalls at a racing stable or crawling under a sheep-shearing shed to rake out the droppings are small indignities that bring great rewards when it comes down to rebuilding tired old garden soils, or creating soils where (almost) none exist.

2

7

Brooming out pig trucks and cow byres is something else again, but the evidence of even these is soon fixed by a hot shower and soap. And then there is the glorious muck to deal with.

Working one section at a time, follow this pattern of labour. First grub out any really pernicious woody weeds such as blackberry brambles or treat them individually with a systemic, glyphosate-based poison painted onto the stumps. This uses a minimum of poison, though even this will be more than some find acceptable. Each one needs to work through the issues for themselves. Testing and public health authorities assure us glyphosates self-destruct on contact with the soil and that the by-products are safe, but there are many who find little comfort in industrial self-regulation or the supervision of regulatory bureaucrats. So the best course of action will be

Adobe clay soil at Buena Creek, California made productive through years of mulching and composting

personal investigation, discussion and decision making. Having by one means or another, removed the most difficult, persistent perennial weeds, lay the saved newspapers over the patch being worked. Some advocates suggest as few as four sheets thickness of paper, but that seems rather insubstantial and a little too prescriptive. If you have broadsheets, just use the wads of folded pages that make up the sections; they should be about right and, like all newspapers, they can be adjusted for balance. Tabloids require a little more work to give the same coverage, and obviously Saturday editions will be a great, especially if the paper used comes from a large city or is a national daily. The quality of the reporting is of small consequence to the end product, but the quality of the paper is important; more particularly it should not contain large amounts of colour printing for the dye-stuffs contain unknown ingredients which may counteract building good soil. Now, before the wind starts to blow and before the neighbours begin to 'phone the local authorities about the unsightly rubbish dump that

it appears is being created within sight of their patio, wheel out the barrowloads of mulching stuff. That will really set expectations that the neighborhood tone is about to slide. Spread the mulch about thickly until not one speck of newspaper can be seen; spread it as thickly as possible with no thought of saving some for the next patch and plan to get more. Lots more. If the mulching materials include large leaves that are likely to blow about, endeavour to anchor them with an thin overlay of some heavier stuff such as lawn clippings. Likewise straw and pea straw can be kept in place until the whole has settled into an interknit thatch. Dogs, blackbirds and cats can be a problem with their predeliction for digging and scatching. The mulch can get disturbed, mounded-up or scattered across pathways and over plants. To prevent this and to discourage animals use 'pegs' of twigs or bamboo pushed through the mulch and the newspaper down into the soil to hold everything in place.

A thick mulch of gravel and wood chips encourages Astelia chathamica and an Eriogonum sp. in a car park at Mendocino, California.

A drenching from a hose will help to weigh the mulch and paper down long enough for it to settle. Should the weather be hot and dry, a hosing every day for a week should set things to rights.

Once the mulch has settled, planting can begin. To do this, gently part the

2
9

mulch by hand, cut a slash through the paper and make a planting hole. Sprinkle in a handful of pelleted manure; plant the plant, push back the paper and mulch, and water thoroughly. It is a good tip to scratch a shallow, water-catching well in the dirt around the plant so that any water given to the plant is soaked into the plant's root zone.

This all sounds, and is, pretty easy, but do not be fooled by anyone into thinking that a maintenance-free garden has been achieved. It has not. The mulch must be replaced as it rots away. The work can be repeated every six months or so, or it can be treated as a more or less continuous process by constantly adding compostable stuff to the top of the mulch. The critical point is that the mulch must be replaced year in, year out if the soil is to benefit. The process is cyclic and never-ending and should become a part of regular, routine garden work. By the time the second helping of mulch has been added to the soil, consideration could be given to adding earthworms to assist the soil building, that is if there is not already a healthy population of them already at work.

Is this a 'no-dig' method of gardening and soil building? Yes. Does it follow any guru? No. It seems like a plain commonsense approach to gardening that could be summarised by saying 'Don't do work that is not necessary and use whatever suitable materials can be had for the most reasonable cost'. This is, of course, with the usual caveats about due care and keeping an alert eye on progress.

But what of my friend in British Columbia attempting to make a garden on a mountainside in a soil, if it could be called that, of rock shards, shales and screes? The method that works for me on my gentle slope would be impossible for her without some prior work. Should she wish to clothe the arid talus with greenery, the task is billy-goat's work scrambling up and down and across the skiddery, skuttery rocks to excavate semicircular mini-terraces; one for each plant. But should a useful garden space suitable for walking, eating outdoors, playing or growing a flower garden be her choice, terraces are the back-breaking answer. The lady who created the Burchart Gardens near Victoria, British Columbia, related to some reporter how she had swung over her quarry in a bosun's chair to plant the cliffs of the quarry walls. But she was a lady of some considerable determination to take on quarry gardening in the first place. Think of her dangling over the rock-face connected by a thin steel hawser to an ancient chugging steam winch.

I think my friend may not have the grit for such an enterprise, or the equipment. She won't need crampons, ropes or an alpenstock, but with a pick, some stout flat-soled shoes and a good sense of balance she can cautiously begin to excavate planting holes along the rocky slopes. As I've seen it done, the holes are dug so that about half of the hole is cut into the slope and the other half is mounded up against the lower side of the slope to make a planting hole that is half-in and half-out of the hillside with a flat, or slightly concave surface for planting on. Each hole is liberally laced with rich compost as it is prepared so as to give plants as good a start as possible, and when planting is finished a miniature version of the above method of mulching is constructed around the plant and to the rim of the excavation. The whole lot, plant, mulch, paper and compost are drenched with a water. As before, the mulch needs to be replaced on a regular basis and can be supplemented with compost and clumps of weeds, their roots shaken free of dirt and left to dry, die and rot as a kind of free-style mulch. A gardener I met once in New Zealand, Ann Endt — garden assistant to Nancy Steen — used the unmarketable, matted dag-ends of sheeps' fleeces to knit her hillside mulches together. It worked brilliantly; a classic example of free-style mulching with whatever is available and affordable. Building up rocky soils in difficult situations by this means is hard work, but it is almost nothing in comparison with the Herculanean efforts needed to terrace a hillside.

Terracing is probably not the sort of thing that sane folk take on single-handed. In days of yore when entire, and large, families could be called on to spend a few days picking rocks off a field, while the men-folk turned them into drystone walls, it may have seemed a small step or two upward in skills and knowledge to turn such rocks into terrace walls. However, even farm workers in the post-Industrial age were beginning to lose the ability to build such things; rural skills were already becoming the province of academic artisans of the arts and crafts movement. Nowadays, to build a drystone wall it is imperative to attend a full semester course at a technical college; to build a terrace wall, a full architectural degree with majors in heritage conservation and primitive construction techniques is probably needed. Then there are those who can operate a bobcat and backhoe.

Modern landscapers have fallen for all manner of pre-fabricated, lightweight construction techniques to build retaining walls, but these seem unsatisfactory for a number of reasons: the materials have a finite life; to optimise the lifespan of the materials, walls have to be built with a deep backfill of course gravel and rocks; such walls are difficult to plant successfully and are even more difficult to keep watered; and terrace walls such as these lack the substantial presence of a stone wall. Aesthetically, they are most impoverished, devoid of visual and tactile interest and not a suitable home for plants. A skillful backhoe operator can move around the largest rocks and small boulders to construct a very sound wall, and with the equipment also be able to

3

1

*Salvias,
rosemaries
and other
hardy sub-
shrubs make a
pleasing
combination in
this Palo Alto,
California
garden.*

back-fill with soil. Given a degree of willingness to cooperate, such a person can be given direction about the placement of the rocks to make a wall that will match any ancient terrace. Be warned however, that what has been described here is not an easy thing to achieve; every back-hoe operator has passed a postgraduate course in cut-and-fill techniques, and that is almost certainly what they will want to do — cut a slice of rocks and shale out of your problematical hill-side and shove it around to make a platform of rock and shale to fill in the downside of your slope. What this creates for your amusement and masochistic gratification is a flat ground of rock and shale ... a garden, never!

Take a moment to visualise a genuine rock garden and then pick your contractor carefully. Bear in mind that I am speaking here of real earthworks, rather than a low retaining wall to hold back a bank a metre or less high. For this purpose, railway sleepers and other contrivances may serve well enough, but for major cut and fill operations on slopes and hillsides heavy, weight-bearing construction is required and this is where stonework comes into its own.

Every day I drive down a freeway through hills to the city. The last bend in the road is marked by a splendid wall of stone which holds back a high bank of earth formed to screen noise and light from an adjacent development. The wall has been made of massive freestone rocks, each carefully chosen and closely fitted together by a very skilled artisan mason using a bob-cat and his own good eye for natural design. The massive stones in the base of the wall remind me strongly of the ancient Inca walls that are found in Lima. They are not nearly so finely fitted, but their mass and geometry suggest links with an age-old tradition in which a feeling for the intrinsic qualities of the material being used was reflected in the way it was used. As yet the wall has no plants, not even weedy opportunists like fennel, oats or artichokes. The scale of the thing calls out for one or two clumps of tall, spiky yucca; perhaps a fat, round-leaved prickly pear or a mat of saltbush; maybe a ceanothus or manzanita trailing down from the top — not so much growth as to detract from the power of the stones, but enough to highlight the massive weight of the thing. Such a wall commands attention and needs sensitive planting. Oh, for the chance of it.

My friend in Italy has a problem somewhat similar to that which could eventuate should a contractor have his way with a back-hoe as described above. His ground is flat and rock-filled. In his case it is also filled with assorted scrap-iron, decaying Fiats, tractor tyres and megalitres of sump oil, and surrounded by the high walls of his neighbours' artisan homes. Not a promising site for a garden, though a real estate developer might take it on as a slum clearance and sell it off as an up-market post-Industrial artists' colony. But they would still have a problem about what to do with the soil just as those who 'garden' in asphalted yards do, and do those whose ground is pure rock. No gardener would ever choose to make a garden on such unfortunate sites, but sometimes real estate values make such things necessary. Pot gardening may be an answer for such situations, but there is another answer that was developed and refined into a system of

Plectranthus argenteus is well suited to dry conditions and light shade.

3
3

gardening by Esther Dean of Sydney. The idea is to create a kind of instant garden bed on top of the ground by laying down whole bales of pea-straw or oaten straw to make a garden bed. The top is liberally spread with a layer of compost and the whole lot, sides and all, covered in old carpet squares, worn-out Honnan matting, large cardboard boxes disassembled and spread out or a thick layer of old newspapers. Bricks, cement building blocks, car tyres — anything heavy — are used to weigh the garden down so it won't blow about or be dislodged from its spot. Rather like a dry-land version of the floating gardens made on beds of willow boughs and reeds that drift around in Lake Dal in Kashmir.

Plants are set directly into the top of the beds by slashing through the compost and straw, inserting a tomato, pepper, eggplant or whatever, and nudging in some of the compost around the roots. Heavy watering settles things in and starts the decomposition process. The relatively impervious outer skin of old carpet etc. limits the loss of water and 'goodies', and keeps the compost at a comfortable temperature for the young plants to grow and for the micro-flora to work on making compost out of the straw. Unlike the hot-beds of fresh manures that were used to grow cucumbers and melons, and even bananas and pineapples, in 19th century gardens, the idea here is to keep the soil cool rather than hot. This system works well for annual vegetables and flowers, but would be more difficult for plants that need sustaining over years. No doubt with determination and ingenuity at least some shrubs and perennials could be accommodated. The resultant garden doesn't always look much like a proper garden; more like a hippie garden, a bit strange, rough around the edges, recycled and biodegradeable. And so it should.

Not far from my home is the Barossa Valley, an area famous for its wines; the valley floor is a patchwork of vineyards, market gardens, orchards and small towns and hamlets with Germanic names. On the eastern crest of the valley, a series of small vineyards has been blasted out of the hillsides to make cooler, high-altitude *steingarten*. The idea was to replicate, as nearly as possible, the steep-sided vineyards of the Rhine Valley and to grow grapes that would produce Rieslings of great finesse. The descendants of the German religious refugees who settled in the valley in the 1840s quite naturally look to German wine styles as their model and hence their creation of the 'stone-gardens'. The deep litter of shales that resulted from the blasting serves two purposes in the vineyard; it conserves ground water against evaporation by keeping the soil cool, and later in the grape-growing season reflects both warmth and light onto the ripening clusters. For an *avant garde* gardener with an eye for the sculptural qualities of 'scaping the land, a garden made with a thick layer of pebbles or gibbers for a base could be quite exciting to see, and to make.

In a climate not the least like those we are speaking of in these pages, one such garden has been made on a deep bed of gravel at Denmans, near Fontwell in Sussex. And although it is a very beautiful garden filled with very interesting plants, many from climates akin to our own, it is a garden at its peak in high summer; one which is open to the skies to get all the warmth it can. As it doesn't seek the relaxed restfulness, shade and quietude of a summer garden that is semi-dormant, its potential as a guide lies in the adventurous way its maker, Joyce Robinson, explored the world of plants to give life to her vision, and in the way the garden offers proof that a garden with sheets of gravel, pebbles, cobbles instead of sheets of lawn can hold its own. I wonder if Mrs Robinson would recognise any potential in a well-cultivated *steingarten*, bare of any plants but vines and hot and dusty under a summer sun? Maybe the roadside weeds would strike some chords, for she would recognise the bronzy purple fennel, the artichoke, evening primroses and sundry verbenas.

Denmans is definitely not a 'Xeriscape' — in fact or in its capacity to stimulate our imaginations. Even without one summer flower, the bold masses of plants such as yucca, grasses, ivies, umbellifers, brooms and crucifers united with sheets of silvery leaved plants — herbs, thistles, onions, thymes, lavenders and a host of others — show observant visitors how foliage alone can be exciting. Humpy, bumpy tussocky shrubs and shrublets from the shores of the Mediterranean and California form a background while hither and yon light-framed trees and shrubs from South Africa, Australia and New Zealand push out from the crowded borders or pop up in the foreground, giving height and depth to the whole. Such a means of growing plants in England ensures good drainage and the gravel acts as reservoir of heat on frosty nights and chilly days. Underneath the gravel lies a high water table and real soil.

In the warm, dry scenario we are trying to deal with, the gravel would act to keep soil temperatures cool relative to the air temperature, and undersurfaces of the stones would act as condensation sites for whatever meagre soil moisture there might be. Lack of real soil underneath the gravelly surface layer would make soil enrichment and building a prime consideration. The mulching and surface composting ideas would seem difficult to accommodate in these circumstances, especially where fires are a risk in summer and the mulch, if allowed to dry out, could add to the combustible material. One solution would be to spread a layer of surface compost and mulch at the end of the hot, dry, high-fire-risk season so that it can break down and be worked on by bacteria

3
5

and worms over the cool, wet seasons. The idea is that it would be largely broken down by the time the next dry season arrives. To encourage a more speedy breakdown than would occur naturally, the mulching material should be put through a garden shredder before it is used. Perhaps a better solution would be to make the compost along conventional lines in some out-of-the-way corner and use it lavishly when setting out new plants in holes specially prepared with it. When planting has been completed, the surface layer of gravel can be spread back to cover up the soil with a stony mulch. Later feeding may have to be done using pelletised manures, but I suspect the rate of soil building would be intolerably slow, even for the most patient of gardeners — slower than the time it takes a good *'Steingartenwein'* to mature.

Just as difficult as gardening in gravel in a warm, dry climate is gardening on sand, particularly at the seaside where a limited range of plants adapted to the conditions adds to the limitations imposed by very deficient soils. Building up the soil must be a priority before drawing up plans and buying plants. A deep litter mulch of seaweed, straw, manures, sawdust and whatever else can be had is the best way to go and must be complemented with all the compost that can be made from household waste and with a regular topping-up of the mulch as it disintegrates and is incorporated with the sand. The humus that results from adopting this gardening habit of continuous soil building is vital to water retention near the surface of the soil where plants can use it. If satisfaction can be had from planting deep-rooted plants which can reach down to the water stored deep in the sand, soil building may not be so important, but if a garden is wanted with a greater variety of plants, and with a dense cover of plants over the ground, some enrichment and water conservation must be practised to support the change in balance between available water, plants and soil.

Sandy soils are most often described as 'hungry' and 'lean', which are positive-sounding terms for miserable and mean. Whatever sort of garden is made on sand — from richly planted and water dependent to something more closely imitating nature — the soil will need continuous feeding and building if anything more than the natural flora is desired.

A small pool at Denmans shows how a little water can go a long way.

A letter from a traveller and amateur archeologist now living in England described an ancient Israeli method of conserving water in the soil by constructing shallow crescent-shaped depressions surfaced with small rocks. The rocks served to retain moisture in much the same way as the examples described earlier. It is thought the Israelis used these rock pockets for cultivating olives. A garden grove made of such rocky crescents, each with a tree and some simple, tough plant such as prostrate rosemary, rock rose or lavender cotton with a few freesias, babianas or grape hyacinths or other small bulbs would make a strong visual impact and make a unique solution for garden making on a gentle slope. The opportunities for making gardens that have such strong sculptural qualities are often overlooked. Most often we see and read of plants being used for their sculptural and architectural impact of geometry, bulk, form and volume; how much more exciting gardens could be if the surface of a garden were given the sense of movement and lively animation that this type of treatment would provide. What opportunities for exploring new ideas! To move around not only the plants of a garden to make new combinations, but to move also the surface, suggests some links to the experimentations of artists exploring mixed media. There need be no stodgy, stale solutions to our problems in gardening if we are awake to the widest possible range of ideas.

Focusing water to the roots of plants where it is needed in this way has been taken one step further in another ancient technique, still used in the Canary Islands and some other parts of the Mediterranean. On the volcanic hillsides of the Canaries and nearby Madeiras, vignerons and farmers of other bushy crops form inverted cones in their soil and line them with rocks of light lava pumice. The effect of these is to concentrate rainfall at the roots of the plants and to keep soil moisture there for use in the dry season. The sight of a field constructed in this way creates the sensation of being in an exotic lunar landscape. Curiously, a very similar method of garden construction occurred to the Maoris early in their settlement of New Zealand so the idea has a widespread currency. In this case, they wished to create drainage and heat traps for their crops of kumara (sweet potato), so while the Maoris' application was reverse to that of the Canarians, the construction was virtually the same.

For the purposes of making a striking garden, the moonscape could be carried further with a planting of silvery-leaved plants. For startling 'Modernism', a formal scheme could be worked out that harks back to the highly stylised geometric gardens designed by Gabriel Guvrekian and admired by Christopher Tunnard (*Gardens in the Modern Landscape*, 1938). Such ideas won't suit everyone, so a softer approach to the same idea could be to swathe the bold structure under an overlay of subtle planting using low creepers, grasses and bold foliage plants to accentuate the highs and lows of the novel landscape. Consideration of where shadows fall and their movement during the day could add drama to a garden built this way, especially if plants of bold silhouette and stature were placed where moving shadows would accentuate the undulating surface of the garden. Varying the scale af such earthworks could offer tree-sized depressions to work with, or something much smaller and set with jewels of the plant world.

Political correctness is much talked of these days, and while not generally thought to include gardening among its subject fields, when it comes down to it there are plenty of rigid purists who hold that there is only one way to design, make compost, select plants or control pests and diseases. They rabbit on loudly and at length about living in harmony with nature, or about the fight with nature. From either blinkered perspective they cannot see or admit how boring they can be, or how their polarised views do not help us to develop a middle way between being the root cause of all our problems with environment and being the answer to all our problems with the natural world.

Those of us who make gardens in warm, dry climates and who are faced with ancient soils of sand and grit, or with newer soils of shales and rocks, must do all we can to build our soils disregarding the metaphysics and mumbo-jumbo espoused by a few. Our designs, choice of plants and management of our gardens must grow out of exploring all possible ideas, not with the idea of staying where we are but of moving forward in all aspects of our gardening. If we don't we shall always be stuck among the rocks and other hard places.

3
9

L E T   S P R I N G S   O F

fresh water

R I S E

I R R I G A T I N G   G A R D E N S   I N   W A R M ,   D R Y   C L I M A T E S

To get down to the nitty-gritty please turn to page 43. If you can't be bothered with reading at all, the diagrams begin on page 46, but if you are in no particular hurry and can take time to relax and enjoy the discomfiture of a non-technical gardener, read on.

If we are to believe the advertising media, watering gardens in a manner that keeps them green and growing, and that conserves water by delivering only what is needed direct to the roots, is simply a matter of installing drippers and spray-jets. It seems as simple as pie. So easy, in fact, that any home gardener can, in one spring afternoon, set in place an entire automated garden watering system. Or so it is said. And there are home handymen who build ferro-concrete ocean-going yachts in their backyards too! And then there are the rest of us. Plain booby that I am, I bought the home watering kit (without the automatic timer — I know my limitations) and set

Previous pages:

(p. 40) Nolina, echium and other dry-climate plants help to create the magic of the 19th century gardens at La Mortola, near Ventigmilia on the Italian Riviera, and

(p. 41) Lampranthus spectabilis, ice plant.

about putting it in. Half the garden was dug up us I sought to lay those easily installed black poly-plastic pipes; neither tree roots nor subterranean wiring stayed my pick and shovel work across the lawn, and cement paths and driveways were no obstacles to my inexpert sapping techniques. Angle joints, end stops, T-junctions and risers saw me master corners and changes in level, scale sheds and tunnel under drains. I felt quite an expert; it looked almost professional, and when I connected it up to a tap, water dripped and sprayed appropriately from each tiny outlet. An opportune time to shout a chorus of 'Glory be to de Lawd' and break out the champagne. A rare case of truth in advertising! The gadgetry did actually water the garden and it was easy, and it did take only one afternoon — and a technological dud like me could do it.

It did *seem* that I had the problem of watering the garden licked. Everything went along nicely for the first summer; water was applied to the roots of the plants, they grew and flowered in a fine display. Despite the heatwaves and the drought the whole garden looked in great condition. But then came the water bill; we had not saved any water at all. In fact, we had used a good deal more. Thinking it over, I rationalised that the water was spent in establishing many new plants that would in future need no watering. A letter of explanation to the water supply authority produced not the expected rebate for community mindedness, but a stern rejoinder that our water meter had been accurately read and that a test of the meter for accuracy would be at our expense. So we went into the next summer prepared to be much harder on our plants and much smarter in the way we applied water to the garden. Without our knowing it, the foolproof irrigation system had a few water-saving tricks we did not expect. Once the summer drought got into stride we found the watering system when turned on produced only a dribble of water from each spigot and sprinkler. Even at full force the water just trickled out. Plants began to flag. And tempers began to rise when it was realised that the whole assembly was blocked up with silt and spiders' webs and pine needles and dead millipedes and other minute flotsam and jetsam. Each fine jet and outlet had to be poked clean with a needle, rinsed out and returned to its place. It took hours of backbreaking work. Our local hardware store suggested fitting a small filter near the tap would fix the problem. As the water passed through the filter all the small grit and detritus would be trapped and only pure water would pass through the pipes to the outlets at each plant. It would be simple to take off the filter every now and then, squirt it clean with a hose and put it back. It was too, but it did not make any difference to the pine needles, the spider webs or the dead insect life; they get into the system from the outlets, not through the water supply. It was a hard lesson to learn, but there are no easy ways to water a garden, unless it can get by on that which falls from the sky — and that can be pretty unreliable when it is most wanted. There are ways which require different sorts of work and maintenance — input, I guess the experts would call it. Trickle, drip and mini-jet spray systems need regular cleaning out to ensure that blockages don't render the entire set-up inoperable. If you choose hoses and sprinklers instead there is the back-bending hump and haul to heave the hefty gear across lawns and beds without damage to plants. And then there is a clock to be watched. But neither of these answers to the question of how to provide water to a garden really addresses the main consideration — how to use water in a conservative manner. How to cut down on water use in gardens; now there is the real problem. Using less water is the crunch issue.

To save water in a garden you have to use less of it. Obvious isn't it? What is less obvious is the inescapable fact that this means that many of the water-dependent plants that gardeners love, the old favourites that are attached by sentiment to our cultural roots and to family histories, have to go. In warm, dry climates the entire garden cannot be green and flowery all summer long if water is to be saved. High summer colour from beds of annuals, dahlias, delphiniums, roses and fuchsias and perennial borders demand too much water; high floral performance comes at the cost of high water consumption. Expanses of green grass under a merciless, hot and powerful sun burning in a cloudless sky must have liberal quantities of water every few days to stay green.

So let us be plain about it: to save water in summer, things will have to change; we will have to use less water on our gardens in the hottest months and we will have to grow different plants to those now so prevalent. We will have to develop new ideas about gardens to maintain our surroundings as a pleasant environment for our homes. This sounds pretty dogmatic. It is, but better perhaps that we should make these changes gradually and in our own time, coming to terms with the need to conserve water, than to have some member of government smarmily pontificating about 'water awareness' as the price of water is hiked yet again, and our gardens are let die in order to keep within the household budget.

To use less water in irrigating a garden need not mean using less water everywhere. A garden of cactus and succulents may need much less water, but it may also be thought too bizarre and grotesque for wholesale adoption in the suburbs; likewise suburb after suburb of gardens of xerophytic native plants could be so desperately dull and monotonous that they too would be thought barren and uncivilised. A more acceptable approach to garden making could be to settle on a balance of high, moderate and low water use areas in each garden. A small area of high

4

3

water use garden may be maintained in some key area of the garden such as a lawn for toddlers to play on, or a group of summer flowers by an important focus point such as a doorway or gate. A somewhat larger area could be assigned to growing plants which need only a little supplementary watering to see them safely through a summer drought, and the remainder of the land available for garden making should be given over to plants which can prosper year round with no irrigation. At first thought the idea occurs that a garden laid out on this principle would resemble a series of roughly concentric zones where the highest water-use zone would be at the centre of the garden and the lowest water-use area would be on the perimeter, with the moderate-use section as a belt between. Following up this concept, the high water-use part would be the smallest area and the no water-use part would be the largest. For planning purposes, this idea may be useful, especially to beginners who have no familiarity with the diversity of plants that will flourish in warm, dry climates. However, other layouts are possible where the high and medium use sectors are used as islands of special plants surrounded by a base planting of no-water-use garden.

This is a water-efficient garden; one where water is delivered without wastage to the plants that need it. This is a water-conserving garden; one where plants are chosen with regard to their water requiremets. This is an climatically sensitive garden; one where the patterns of growth match the pattern of the seasons. This is an engaging home landscape; one where a setting has been created that fits the house to its surroundings. This is an exciting garden, for in making it the gardener has had to explore the world of plants to identify and obtain plants outside the mainstream available in garden centres.

This is all very well and straightforward for those who garden where town water is available, but what of those who garden in areas where there is no reticulated domestic water supply? What indeed? How do they manage? Where can water be had? Perhaps things are not always as simple as they seem to writers and garden makers of highly urbanised consumer societies.

It happens that in many parts of the Old World, agriculture has long relied on rainfall run-off being stored in reservoirs, or by water being channelled from streams, and delivered to the farmers' fields according to a strict rotation. Water rights are a very valuable commodity, and the stuff itself so precious that it seems an incredible waste to use it in making flower gardens. Farmers know such things. It just isn't right to water flowers when it could be used to grow wheat or vegetables, or to irrigate vines, fruit trees or rice. The water rights have been allocated for several centuries perhaps; changing the

rotation and the quantity is a very difficult
thing to do. There must be meetings of
the other owners of rights and their rights
must be respected; there must be meetings
held with the authorities; lawyers must be
called on for advice; the parties should
bargain and the dignity of a farmer's work
must be honoured; the price must be
agreed and the contracts must be signed –
the business of buying water rights goes
on interminably. In Spain, Portugal, parts
of southern France and Italy, water rights
apply in many areas; usually it seems
wherever newcomers want to enjoy the
peace and charm of rural areas by setting
up retirement homes or holiday houses.
While negotiating enough water for
household use may be fairly
straightforward, getting the extra needed
to make a garden (or, heaven forbid, to fill
a swimming pool) can be a protracted
business. Considering the numbers of

such houses in once-rural areas, the strain on limited local water resources must be near
breaking point in many heavily redeveloped resort spots. After all, it is not just the new
home owners that want more water; what about the golf courses and the restaurants and
all the other water-hungry add-ons entailed in such settlements. In the past, it has been
possible for highly water-dependent gardens to be made based on the supplies of water
diverted from agricultural, use but now that profligate use must surely come to an end.
Communities have reached the point where they will have to decide whether it is golf
courses and gardens that get the water, or farms and fields.

On Cyprus, where irrigation water could very easily be in short supply and
drought ruin many farmers, the EOKA (Freedom) troubles between Turkish and Greek
communities early in the 1970s saw many tussles over good farming land and water
supplies as boundaries were disputed and settled. In this case, the irrigation water and tap
water for the house are supplied separately; the gritty irrigation water pumped up from

Utility and
beauty
combined in a
farmyard
setting,
Campsis
radicans *(syn.*
Bignonia
radicans) *scales*
a windmill and
water tower.

4

5

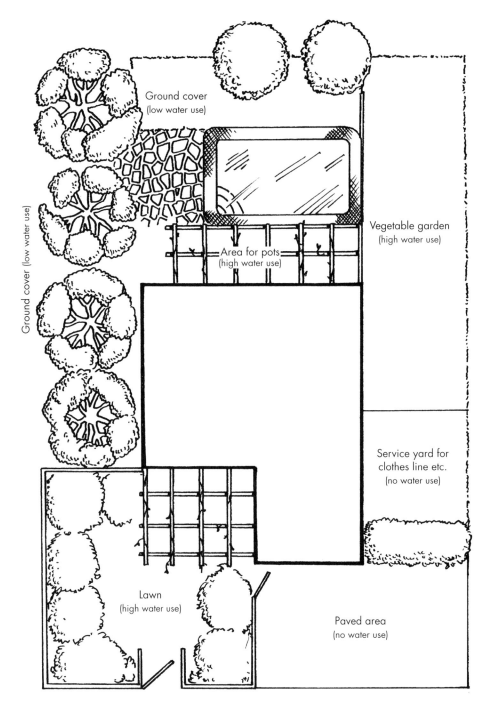

Water use focused in particular zones in the garden with high water use either in important living areas or productive areas.

Ground cover
(low water use)

Ground cover (low water use)

Vegetable garden
(high water use)

Area for pots
(high water use)

Service yard for
clothes line etc.
(no water use)

Lawn
(high water use)

Paved area
(no water use)

deep wells and the tap water carefully stored in reservoirs from snow melt and rains in the inland hills. Each is delivered through a separate, metered system. A correspondent from Papho on the island tells how his family were moved backward and forward as refugees from both warring parties, eventually being settled on farmland that was once

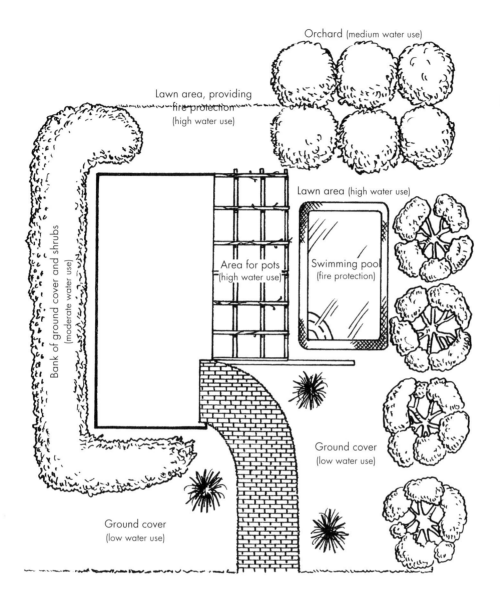

Orchard (medium water use)

Lawn area, providing fire protection (high water use)

Lawn area (high water use)

Bank of ground cover and shrubs (moderate water use)

Area for pots (high water use)

Swimming pool (fire protection)

Ground cover (low water use)

Ground cover (low water use)

Turkish, and very poor rocky stuff at that. By good fortune the World Bank established a water supply scheme as part of the resettlement effort and with hard work and tons of imported red soil, grape skins, seaweed and *kopri* (goat dung) the farmlet now supports carobs, stone fruits, vines, olives and citrus trees and a flourishing flower garden.

The importance of water for irrigation in settlement programs goes back at least to Roman times and perhaps even longer. Scattered around the Mediterranean from Turkey and the Near East to the southern shores in Egypt and Libya, are the remains of Roman soldier settlements founded on water supplies brought in from remote mountains and distant springs. Many failed and were deserted because the water quality

47

deteriorated, becoming excessively saline, or because the source of supply simply became exhausted or was diverted by besieging armies. For them there were no sophisticated trickle irrigation systems or micro-jets or electronic timers, just a simple gravity-fed flow down canals and over aqueducts to sluice gates and fields watered by flood irrigation. With no knowledge of measuring salinity or of counteracting rising salt in the soil, there must have been many more failures than are experienced today. And that is not to say there are no problems in these areas today, but that is another story ...

Less ancient methods of getting water are found in shallow wells fitted with pumps driven by windmills (and now by electricity) and bores which are sunk deep into the earth; the water either coming out by itself under force, or being pumped out by powerful machines. Well water is usually ground water that lies close to the surface and that has

collected in an aquifer of soil or sand as a result of local rainfall. It can usually be tapped easily by simply digging or drilling a short shaft into the earth until the water table is reached. In days gone by, the shaft would have been widened and lined with bricks and a well head and bucket installed at the surface. Now it is usual to install a narrow metal casing (i.e. pipe) that just fits into the drill hole and then to lower down a special 'thin' electrical pump that pumps water out to a storage tank as needed to keep it topped up.

Allium acuminatum, a drought-tolerant bulb that grows and flowers before the heat and drought of summer arrive.

Sounds easy, doesn't it? It is fairly simple until the well runs dry as the water table drops during the hot months, then a deeper well has to be dug until the water table is relocated and the pump lowered until water can be drawn again. The real problem is when every neighbour begins to do the same, especially when some neighbours get serious about water extraction and dig deeper than everyone else and install larger, more powerful pumps. At times of drought when everyone uses water at a high rate, the water table can drop rapidly and take a considerable time to recover its usual level. Eventually there are losers, some bores fail completely or maybe the concentration of dissolved salts and minerals rises, thus spoiling the water and rendering it useless for gardens.

Like most things these days, locating and drilling for water can be a very expensive business, especially when the work is done under the duress of urgent need.

48

Problems can arise and there can be disappointments. Like hatching chickens, finding underground water is best done before any outcomes are presumed. As a first step to deciding whether or not to drill for water, guidance can be sought from a professional water driller who should be able to demonstrate on the geological survey maps (which exist for many areas) the stratum of rock where underground water might lie. Alternatively, recourse might be made to the services of a water diviner; a much more ancient craft and in these scientific times one that appears anachronistic and highly suspect. However, it is often surprising to learn that a water diviner has had success where the more modern, 'scientific' method of locating underground water has failed. Who knows why? Perhaps the diviner has a background of local knowledge and lore that assists in divining. To watch diviners at work is fascinating, especially when their searches are aided by pigs or dogs — it is almost worth the diviner's fee just to see the rustic method and the ancient ritual.

The discovery of water is not of itself guarantee of a green, lush garden. The contractor who digs the well or drills the bore hole will test the water for several things: the presence of solids such as grit and sand, the presence of dissolved salts and minerals, and the rate of flow (litres or gallons per hour) and maybe the pressure of the flow. Dull technology is necessary for the delivery of the precious liquid, even if a water diviner has been employed to find the stuff.

Advice must be taken before a final commitment is made to draw water from underground; the contractor will have some information, but it is also helpful to have the experiences and knowledge of others to draw on when deciding if the water will be potable and/or useful for irrigation, and what sort of plants it will support. Surely water is water, I hear you say. Sadly, no. Sometimes ground water is heavily tainted with substances which make it useless for drinking or irrigating. Before it is brought to the surface in quantity it must be tested; if it is of good quality, plans can go ahead, but if it is tainted or foul it is better left where it is and the drill hole capped, or the well filled in. A water analysis usually shows the presence of sodium salts, carbonates and boron, which all have a critical impact on the soil conditions, on the working parts of the irrigation equipment and on healthy

Euphorbia lathyrus, an annual sub-shrub that self-sows willingly in dry, gravelly soils.

4
9

plant growth. The testing should be done by a reputable commercial laboratory or by the local branch of the government agricultural extension office.

Getting the water 'on tap' requires a properly designed irrigation system to be set up. This would include the well or bore with its pump, a storage tank of some considerable volume; the interconnecting piping valves and inspection points and the distributing network of a filter, pipes, drippers, sprinklers and the like. Most modern systems have an multistation automatic computer-controlled system operated by a combination of soil humidity sensors and time switches with a manual override. Installing such complicated equipment is not a job for home handymen or handywomen. The components are expensive and have to be set up by someone who knows what they are about; the job must proceed in a set sequence, mistakes are costly to repair and time-consuming too. In many countries, the work would have to be done by qualified plumbers and electricians; to have it done otherwise often negates the protection provided by household insurance policies.

'Grey water' is a term that comes up more frequently now that the topic of saving water is discussed more widely in our communities. It is a term that derives from the colour of used household water that was once commonly run outside to the garden to water trees and other plants. The waste water was that which had been used in baths, showers, laundry and dishwashing and contained mostly water, a very small quantity of solids and a small amount of soap. Now that many of us live in homes with deep drainage systems it has become problematical, if not illegal, to divert this grey water for use in the garden. In most of the suburban areas of Australia, California and New Zealand, all household liquid waste must go into sewerage systems, regardless of whether or not it could be safely recycled. Nonetheless, as the costs of domestic water supplies go up and up, many home owners are once again turning to the old-fashioned practice of saving sudsy dishwater and laundry rinse water and using it to water their gardens. Keeping the dirty dishwater and other household water means stopping clothes washers and dishwashers midcycle and siphoning off rinse waters and wash waters directly into the garden, bucketing it from sinks to the garden or running a hose into settling tanks. It means just as much mucking around to save bath water and shower water.

It also means being particular about the kinds of soap and detergent used, so that excess quantities of phosphates and boron are not dumped in the soil. These substances are poisonous to plants. At first they stunt growth; their presence in the soil shows up as reddish discolourations on the leaves and quickly results in the leaves yellowing, browning and falling off. Eventually the plants will die. Over time phosphates and

5
0

GARDENS OF THE SUN

boron, as found in many modern dishwashing and laundry detergents, also act on the soil so that it becomes water-repellent and conglomerated; that is the soil particles stick together in small, water-repellent granules and any water or rain runs straight through the layer of contaminated soil, making it almost impossible to sustain any plant life, even if it is tolerant of the levels of phosphates and boron.

Saving household water also means being more fussy about how fats and oils are disposed of; if the waste water is to go onto the garden, these substances cannot be sloshed down the drain with the water. Not that they should be anyway; congealed cooking fats and oils should not be rinsed off plates and pots but scraped off into absorbent paper and disposed of with other hard rubbish. Even so, a grease trap may have to be devised to remove globules of the gooey goop from waste water before it is used to water plants. Almost as bad as fats are the scraps that get fed into waste disposal systems. Shredded and pulverised vegetable and meat scraps rinsed out to gardens from kitchen sinks quickly turn into a putrid rotten mass that fouls the soil and the air. A better strategy for the vegetable scraps is to keep them apart for including in a compost heap or used to make a 'no dig' mulch; the meaty bits could be used on a worm farm, but the fatty parts must be disposed of in the rubbish bin.

With all these potential causes for bad smells, attracting flies, mosquitoes and rats, infections and fouled soils, it is hardly surprising that our grandparents were so enthusiastic about the benefits of deep drainage which flushed all the wastes of a household out to sea, or to some other waterway a long way from home. 'Out of sight, out of mind' as we so often say was never truer than in the case of these sanitary arrangements. After a hundred years or so of managing liquid household wastes this way, we are beginning to realise that the practice is not without cost to the environment; coastal fishing grounds and beaches are being damaged. The realisation of the negative impact that dumping waste water at sea, or in rivers and lakes can create is now leading civic health and environmental authorities to reconsider how the huge quantities of contaminated water can be reduced.

Separating the grey water from the toilet waste produced by a household can cut the volume of fouled water produced by a large percentage. Planners and designers are now beginning to work out ways of saving, storing and using grey household waste water. Until these problems are resolved, home-based recycling of dirty water from the kitchen and laundry will mean a return to the siphon and the bucket brigade, but it will also mean that we are saving and recycling one of our most precious assets, and it will help us to remember that the best environmental protection begins at home.

5

1

HORTI-cultural BAGGAGE

Do you ever succumb to the temptation to eavesdrop on conversations? I do, particularly those that occur between customers and sales assistants in nurseries and garden shops. I like to consider what my answers to queries might be. I must give myself away by the self-satisfied look on my face for I am sometimes invited to give an opinion on this or that small problem.

It may be perverse, but I get a kick out of the possibility that I might actually know more than the sales person, and that they acknowledge it. Maybe this sensation comes about because the invitation to become an adviser is a chance to get my own back on the plant peddlers for years of hard sell and years of misinformation. You probably know the sort of thing I mean, 'Yes, madam, this azalea is perfectly hardy here in Desert Dunes.' 'No, madam, azaleas do not need special soils and won't need any

PREVIOUS PAGES:

(p. 52) Majestic

Aloe africana

flowers in mid-

winter. It has

been a popular

plant in warm,

dry gardens

since it was

introduced

from the Cape

Province by

settlers sailing

to Australia

the 19th

century, and

(p.53) Agave

parryi

special watering in summer; they grow easily — anywhere!' That sort of sales patter that smooths the way to quick sale and calms our conscience about spending a large sum on a plant that we suspect could die of heat exhaustion tomorrow. A chance to upstage such a spin-doctor's spiel is too hard to pass over.

The topic of one such overheard conversation in a local plant boutique was lavenders. At the counter, between the sprigged cotton chintz garden cushion and the dibber daubed with naive roses, stood a lady complaining about the discrepancies between descriptions of lavender heights. Holding several illustrated labels up to the sales clerk, she wanted to know why the descriptions on the back of the glossy, illustrated plant tag were so different in what they said about plants that appeared to be identical. It is after all reasonable, is it not, to expect that all plants labelled as 'Hidcote lavender' or 'dwarf white lavender' will all be the same? How useful is the same blurb for all varieties. What does the telegraphic 'Sunny, well drained silver purple or white late spring and summer 30 – 60 cm' tell anyone? Why then is the information confusing *and* different *and* uninformative? (I don't expect that question will ever be answered.) And how could she make them into a hedge? Now, it is easy enough to offer advice about sorting this out, should you be asked, and it is possible to offer good advice even if you are not asked, but it is far less easy to question why such plants are wanted in the first place.

Why had the plants to be lavender? Why had they to be Hidcote? The answer, it seems, is that the plants must be lavender and must be the Hidcote form because that is what everyone has. Who is everyone? Well, everyone ... you know; Sissinghurst Castle, Great Dixter, Mottisfont Abbey, Crathes Castle, Cranborne Manor, Bramdean House, Barnsley House, Kiftsgate Court, Hidcote Manor etc.

'These are all English gardeners. Why do you have to have plants used in English gardens?'

'Because Victoria Sackville-West, Christopher Lloyd, Graham Thomas etc. used them. And the pictures in *The English Woman's Garden* and *Sissinghurst: portrait of a garden* are so lovely. It's just what I'm looking for.'

'Why do you have to have what these people recommend? Had you thought of something else, like bush germander (*Teucrium fruticans*).'

'No, I just want Hidcote lavender. Nothing else will give me the right look — and these crazy labels are no help. I *must* have Hidcote lavender and it must grow no more than 30 cm high, exactly as it is in the knot garden at Hatfield House.'

So what is happening in this conversation? The gardens, the plants, the people

— all of them so familiar and all of them held up as unassailable icons. Images, words and knowledge carried far from England to the warm, dry shores of California, the Cape, the 'Med' and Australia. What is happening, and has happened for a very long time; usually ever since Anglo *emigrés* got over their first enthusiasms for whatever garden exotica the native flora may have briefly provided, is that transplanted horticultural traditions were imposed on the possibilities offered by local realities. That such cultural baggage was given the first consideration is not all that surprising. After all, what other information was there by which to make gardens?

What is surprising is that many of our gardening habits and ideas are *still* dominated by those old rituals and beliefs. Why have we not been able to give up those habits and traditions that do not serve us well? Why do we insist still that ideas unsustainable in our climate are the ones to be most eagerly followed? To avoid becoming repetitive and dull, I will not answer my own question again. Instead, allow me to urge my readers: Give up the gardening habits and ideas that do not serve you well; look for plants that will grow well and try new ideas. The pursuit of fashion and 'names' has got us nowhere.

Turning back briefly to the lady at the nursery with the lavender hedge problem, we can see by her example the insidious power of fashion to mould our ideas about how things should be. Had she been able to see the need for a hedge in the light of a challenge to find what plants would suit such a purpose, she would have been able to approach the situation from a different and more productive perspective; what are good hedging materials for Mediterranean gardens? (*Pistacia lentiscus* is one suitable candidate as an alternative to English box [*Buxus sempervirens*] or the much vaunted lavender [*Lavandula angustifolia* 'Hidcote']). Can we make small, low hedges and knots? Can they survive the heat and drought of high summer? Thinking in terms of drought, available soil moisture and root competition, should our hedges be larger and tougher, enclosing decent-sized spaces, making bolder statements. The challenges and excitement offered to Anglo-European gardeners by new settings and climates has a fascinating history — a history that makes absorbing reading and gives rise to a good deal of reflection. What a wonderful thing it must have been at the turn of the century to visit, or better yet own, a garden on the Riviera — French or Italian, what the heck! Travelling back in time to smell the waves of perfume from fields of jonquils and groves of citrus that fed the numerous distilleries and perfumeries and to revel in the luxuriant growth of countless exotic trees, shrubs and climbers would surely eliminate for us, however briefly, any bad memories. Little of that botanic glory and none of the lifestyle to which it was background remains. Standing at the top of the main staircase at La Mortola at the Italian end of the Riviera and looking down the long prospect to the startling blue sea, one cannot help but feel, despite the incredible vegetation that is everywhere about, that it is all rather like an elderly opera diva dressed in outdated costume

jewellery and an outmoded velvet evening gown. The glory has faded, the vibrancy is gone, and yet the presence and bravura remain. The brilliance of the gesture in making the garden, in collecting the plants, cannot be denied by what remains held together by a fragile sense of mystery and the fascination engendered by grotesques. Towering palms, massive tree euphorbias and aloes, monster cereus cacti, enormous strelitzias crowd evergreen oaks and ancient olives; forests of oleander and bauhinia overshadow walks and pools and fountains; groves of eucalypts and thickets of sprawling opuntia block walks and paths and steps. The whole, a fantastic jungle on the verge of taking over completely and swamping forever the man-made terraces, temples and vistas. Looking around it is easy to understand the mesmerism induced by the sight of strange new plants and the compulsion to grow them.

The gardens at La Mortola, and

Lavenders and grasses planted around an old oil jar

others too, may yet be preserved and rejuvenated, but what lesson will they teach us, other than that of the Victorian and Edwardian drive to amass and collect rarities in ever greater numbers. When they were newly planted, teeming with gardeners and fresh with vigorous growth, the cost of their making and the prodigality of their keeping were keenly observed by Lady Paget:

They all spend enormous sums in keeping up sub-tropical vegetation, beds of specimen flowers,

artificial lawns which have to be re-sown every year. Everything about these gardens reeks of money. The best of them attain a theatrical effect with huge palms and roses climbing to their top, shrubs with big flowers, fountains, stone balustrades, and a bit of blue sea or mountain in the distance. There are no drives or walks or resources of any kind within the reach of a moderate income.

In My Tower, *1924*

The crown of thorns, Euphorbia milii *(syn.* E. splendens) *from Madagascar, makes a bright display in frost-free situation.*

In reality, these gardens were just grand extensions of the old models, flower gardening carried further and supported with enormous wealth and vast quantities of piped water.

Fabulously beautiful and near to paradise on earth for the gardening hoi-polloi, they offer a deceptive vision of Eden. These gardens serve only as monuments to a remote, Rothschildian past and as repositories for all kinds of adaptable plants. 'Museum-ism' has its uses, as I hope we will all learn.

The idle rich of the 1880s to the 1920s relocated to the Côte d'Azur for the warmer winters and for their health indulged in planting willy-nilly, running amok with Asian figs, Brazilian bromeliads, South African fig-marigolds, Australian wattles and bottlebrushes. They created gardens of unparallelled magnificence which serve now to highlight for us the benefits of using as wide a palette as possible when making gardens in sunny climates. Who will now show us the benefits of restraint in choosing from that palette?

5
7

There has been another kind of luxuriant seasonal garden too; made by European colonialists going to up-country 'hill stations' for the duration of 'The Hot'. Made in cooler areas of nonetheless warm, dry countries, these gardens also tended to be made in spite of local conditions rather than in acknowledgement of them. It is amusing now to read of the trials and tribulations of Memsahibs and Missies trying to make gardens tended by 'unknowing', 'lazy' native boys, coolies and Burra-wallahs. Directed to make European gardens whatever the climate, regardless of water use, subterranean termites, grazing hordes of locusts, invading hippopotami and nomadic wildebeest, they persisted; accompanied no doubt by giggles and scowls of the locals at the foolishness of their employers. It seems odd now that these efforts did not take into account local expertise and knowledge, preferring instead to persist with knowledge and ideas gained in climates far different to those in force. So strong was the supposed superiority of imported nous that successful local methods were utterly ignored. A sorry story of gardening elitism that is only just beginning to change today.

Has anyone given thought to the appropriateness of water use or of plantings other than those that resemble botanical collections? Of course they must have, but lacking the social *éclat* of the transient millionaires and colonial elites of earlier times, their efforts have thus far remained largely unsung. In the last few years, aided by modern communications and technology and freed from the need to attend to their business in the major capitals, many people from colder parts of Europe have moved south, living permanently around the Mediterranean basin. Some regard themselves as working, others see themselves as semi-retired; many are actively gardening and it is to them — among others in similar climates — that we can look for the first signs of a paradigm shift in the way we think about gardens and the way we make them.

Unlike the earlier group of garden owners who relocated to warm, dry climates for a season, permanent residents eventually realised after varied but frequently lengthy periods of frustration, that the traditional and habitual ways of gardening in cool, temperate climates just do not apply elsewhere.

The transition from one way of gardening to another is not just a simple matter of shifting house and habits from one patch of land in one climatic zone to another in a different climate. Several friends have written of the many frustrations they experienced on moving from England to southern France; one even sent a photograph of herself looking over her terrace garden. Her commentary detailed the difficulties she faced growing familiar 'English' flowers until it dawned on her that she was looking at things from an unhelpful perspective. She felt frustration at the failure of traditional European and American garden flowers; disappointment at finding few hardy, adaptable and attractive plants in nurseries; regret for the uselessness of inapplicable gardening traditions; despair as the heat and drought of long summers sapped the plants despite her best attentions. She endured a malaise induced by the hopelessness of the whole catastrophe. Once she was able to stop pining for an English garden, and gave up trying to practise the garden lore that went with, it she was able to start creating her own style of French garden. The results have been immensely satisfying, though not without some disappointments and the need to rethink some plans. For me the most telling comment of all was that, alongside all the other changes to her life that occurred when she moved permanently to France, changing her gardening habits was perhaps not so hard after all.

Among the other horticultural baggage that some of us may have to overcome in order to garden successfully and happily in Mediterranean-type climates are: the dislike of spiky plants; the dislike of succulent plants; the absolute necessity of winter pruning — particularly for roses; the idea that having many flowers in winter is impossible; the necessity for digging and cultivating; the necessity for making compost as a separate activity; and the idea that to avoid snakes and bushfires, decorative grasses should be banned from the garden. These matters are often declaimed loudly by a certain sector of the gardening world. Not infrequently they will hear no other argument and insist that these views are held by 'all the best gardeners'. It may seem an unfair comment, but it seems to me that their trump card to silence all critics and win the day runs along the lines that 'Of course, it really is impossible to have a decent garden here anyway; no matter what I do nothing could be as perfect as Sissinghurst Castle.' And that gets us right back to where we started.

Well, such perfect squelches deserve the gardens they have and whatever degree of second-rate satisfaction they get from them, but those of us who have thrown off our cultural baggage and released ourselves from old ties are able to move on and discover fresh and exciting aspects of gardening. It would be worth our while to take a look at those few ties above and see why they may no longer apply.

THE DISLIKE OF SPIKY AND SUCCULENT PLANTS

Ugh! Horrid beastly things. This seems a hangover from the days when there was no ready supply of water for irrigating gardens and so to have a garden at all necessitated growing such plants. A case of familiarity breeding contempt, I think. Even the very best English authorities were quite keen on some of these plants. E.A. Bowles was keen on all

Beschorneria yuccoides *from Mexico brightens a Côte d'Azur garden in company with the contrasting foliage of yuccas and agaves.*

manner of spiky things and proudly set out bowls and pots of cactus at key spots in his garden; Miss Jekyll used yuccas so often in her designs that they almost became a trademark; Miss Willmott used huge agaves in tubs so large a donkey was required to cart them into position on her terrace; and Christopher Lloyd admits a sneaking admiration for (and admits to using) sempervivums and sedums in his garden. Beth Chatto, too, makes generous use of sedums and other succulent plants in her garden at White Barn House. With all these 'proper' gardeners lined up in their support, why do succulent plants, with and without spiky bits, find so many detractors? I think the derision can only be derived from a peculiar sort of reverse snobbery. With me, sempervivums and sedums find ready homes in the chinks in dry-stone walls and agaves, aloes and echeverias look welcoming and homely clustered in squat pots on the verandahs of our house.

THE ABSOLUTE NECESSITY OF WINTER PRUNING — PARTICULARLY FOR ROSES

But, Mr Nottle, you must prune roses in June (winter here); don't you agree? Now here is a myth if ever there was one. So far as home gardeners are concerned, almost all pruning can be done whenever there is time to do it. Certainly winter pruning of grapevines and

6
0

deciduous fruit trees seems the most sensible time to train or curtail these plants, however even these can grow and produce reasonable quantities of fruit without pursuing the task rigorously. It is also certain that regular summer pruning and training will significantly reduce the amount of cutting back that may be needed in winter. But shrub roses and most other flowering shrubs can be dealt with immediately after flowering. By choosing shrub roses in preference to the hybrid tea types, the need for winter pruning can be eliminated; modern breeders have significantly increased the flower size and colour range of these roses, so giving a wider choice — almost as wide as that offered by the large-flowered bush roses. As exhibition quality fruits or flowers are not the objective of most home gardeners, there is little need to follow the dictates prescribed by the aficionados of these pursuits.

ABOVE: Aloe saponaria bursts into bloom as the rainy season comes to a close in this garden at Carmel, California.
LEFT: The strong vertical form and acid green colour of Euphorbia canariensis make bold accents in dry, frost-free gardens.

THE IDEA THAT HAVING MANY FLOWERS IN WINTER IS IMPOSSIBLE

This is another myth cemented in the brains of those who genuflect before the superiority of gardening ideals best suited to places other than those with warm, dry climates. What an unhappy crew these folk must be in winter; their flower gardens reduced to jonquils, hellebores, Algerian irises and masses of dormant and semi-dormant plants, and the dire awfulness of unrelenting plantations of laurustinus (*Viburnum tinus*) and photinia (*Photinia serrulata*). Once awake to the possibilities of winter-flowering plants such as correas, wattles, hardenbergias, prostantheras, grevilleas, brachycome, aloes, leucodendrons and proteas, the winter need never be dull or flowerless.

63

THE NECESSITY FOR DIGGING AND CULTIVATING

One of the great myths of gardening is that it cannot be done 'properly' unless the soil is constantly dug and cultivated. Experience shows that this ain't necessarily so. Some parts of a garden may need intensive cultivation, e.g., a vegetable garden where there are annuals to be grown, harvested or rotated, but many parts can happily be left so long as the plants growing in those undug parts are mulched, fed and watered sufficiently to maintain healthy growth and flowering. Esther Dean and others have shown that even vegetables can be grown very well using 'no dig' techniques. This realisation brings with it the idea that composting on the spot with mulches of layered newspapers, vegetable scraps and leaves, and straw works well in warm, dry climates. And it obviates the necessity for making compost as a separate activity. Am I sounding too dogmatic? Perhaps so. If compost is needed for other garden activities such as growing potted bulbs and flowering plants, then of course it must be made. I would be the last person to deny anyone the joy of a compost heap!

THE IDEA THAT DECORATIVE GRASSES BRING SNAKES (AND BUSHFIRES)

This looks like a purely colonial conceit; one that was fine when grasses were 'out' and everyone who gardened seriously wanted to grow delphiniums and dicentras; not growing grasses had a strong base in self-evident commonsense. Times have changed. Now grasses are *de rigeur*, few self-respecting gardeners would be without them. (Be warned, though, about the all too willing Restionaceae family, which can take over.) Given the usual care and attention to removing dead growth, the risk of conflagration can be minimised. As to snakes, I doubt they are any more attracted to grasses than to any other form of plant life. Country gardeners should be careful of thrusting their hands, or unshod feet and bare legs into any sort of plant growth — in a garden or not. So far as I know there are not yet any behaviour management programs that teach snakes the difference between gardens, paddocks and bushland. Snakes sunbake wherever they wish, so make plenty of noise as you go about gardening and trust that the generally retiring habits of snakes will see them slither off well in advance of your approach. Miss Willmott had one gardener on her staff at Warley Place who kept a mongoose; these are reputed to hunt snakes and kill them. In the likely absence of such a useful reptile deterrent I think it entirely possible that you can still enjoy grasses in your garden with little to fear from death adders, rattle snakes or tiger snakes.

And while I am about it, I may as well drag out a few other furphies — and endeavour to knock them on the head.

BROWN IS BAD

And its converse theorem, green is good. This relates to having grass and lawns in the main and springs from the concept that gardens should be lush and green all summer long — regardless of what may be happening in the locality where you live. As the last few summers have shown, even the grass in the most perfect English gardens can go brown. For some the vision splendid was at risk, gardens open to tourists poured water onto the withering green velvet and hoped that a greenish shade of yellow would be convincing; others with a more practical bent — and none too subservient to the vision — decreed that yellow grass would be just fine. Instead of worrying about the grass, which would of course come back green as ever with a shower or two, these sensible folk thought of how the 'warm, dry' season would ripen precious bulbs to flower the better next spring, and enjoyed a rare season of *floraison* from cold-tender subtropical shrubs. Let us enjoy our summer's heat and dry conditions for the pleasure of resting in the shade and for the flowers it will engender in other seasons.

SHAGGY IS BAD – NEAT IS NICE, NEATER IS NICER STILL

Another hoary old *mot juste*, whichever aspect, negative or positive, you care to take. All very well in days gone by when *everybody* had masses of gardeners, weeding boys and such like help to keep every plant in its allocated place and manicured with daily nipping back, pinching out and dead-heading, but now impossible and anyway quite a distraction from the beauty of a garden. We all enjoy the sight of the fat seed capsules of love-in-a-mist, the pearly orange hips of 'Mme Gregoire Staechelin', the trails of *Convolvulous sabatius* (syn. *C. mauretanicus*) that creep across paths and edgings, and the multitudes of plants that seed themselves carelessly into cracks and crannies – all these and more incidents, unplanned by the gardener but delightful. I like the way Derek Jarman put it:

>'If a garden isn't shaggy, forget it.' (*Derek Jarman's Garden*)

Or, should you need an even more powerful justification for 'shagginess' in your garden, you may answer criticisms or personal anxiety over it by remembering Victoria Sackville-West, who said of her gardeners Pamela Schwerdt and Sibylle Kreutzberger: 'They're wonderful girls, but they're too tidy.' If VSW sought a degree of untidiness, you most certainly may have it.

Let us put all this horticultural baggage behind us. There is much to do in discovering how to garden in warm, dry climates, wherever we live, and we do not need the hindrances of old ways of thinking and doing which do not serve us well.

6

3

T R A V E L L I N G   W I T H
ideas

'Who do you think you are, coming here and telling us how to garden?', or gentler words, but to the same effect, and aimed at me when I occasionally sally forth to give garden talks. I dare say there will be some readers who feel much the same way. 'Who is this person telling us to change what we are doing?' I never set out to confront my audiences, and I am fairly confident that I rarely do.

What I do want for my listeners and readers is not that they will be scandalised by what I say, nor even that they will actually change how they garden. What I want is for them to at least think about what they see and what they hear and what they read, and reflect on what they do themselves. And then, perhaps, decide on some new directions for their gardening to take. If I am able to stimulate that chain of events by what I say and show then I can feel satisfied.

PREVIOUS PAGES:

(p. 64) Derek
Jarman's
garden at
Prospect
Cottage near
Dungeness in
Kent is an
object lesson
in how
creative
gardening in
an 'impossible'
situation can
make a world
of difference,
and (p. 65)
Echinocactus
grussonii, *the*
golden barrel
cactus.

Travel is one of the best ways to stimulate fresh perspectives, but dropping our everyday lives and dashing off to the furthest corners of the globe to see plants and visit gardens is not something many of us are able to do. So we must resort to books and magazines, and increasingly to television, to provide us with new experiences, albeit limited by the lens of the camera and the eye of the editor. And, if we are lucky, travel becomes an occasional supplement to our sources of ideas.

As in most other aspects of life, this dependence on visions captured by others in words and pictures has two sides; we are able to bring new ideas and plants to our garden making, and we can also be seduced by what we read and see into thinking that a direct copy of what is before us in a book, or on a screen, will be the answer for our own situations.

As a garden designer, I have had a small career and I am glad for that because I have ample time to write and read and visit gardening friends and I do not have to answer to the call of that all too numerous clan of 'gardeners' who swoop on garden designers and landscapers armed with a copy of *Casa Vogue, Architectural Digest, World of Interiors* or *Maison et Jardin*, point to a glossy full-page colour picture of some idyllic garden and say with a ten-teeth smile, 'I want this'. (I use the term 'gardener' in the broadest possible sense, i.e., they don't actually do it, indeed are most probably incapable but want the effects anyway. Tomorrow.) What can the hapless designer or maker say but 'How many dozens of 'Hidcote' lavender will I order?' After all, bills must be paid, a roof kept over one's head and food set on the table. With competition for commissions so strong, there are very few designers who would dare to suggest that Madam, or Sir, might care to consider the wisdom of copying a garden made in another place under very different conditions. It would take a brave heart simply to suggest that a potential client may like to talk through how the particular attributes of the garden pictured would assist what is now contemplated. The likely reaction would be for the client to spurn the designer and take his or her business elsewhere. What needs to be understood is that in cases like this the client is not seeking attributes that answer needs any more than they are seeking a garden designed to meet the singular requirements of their lifestyle and the prevailing conditions of the site. No, what is wanted by customers of this demanding variety is the purchase of an image. They want an image that will reflect and support the image they have of themselves, and the one they want others to think of them as having. To be fashionable is what they want, nothing more, and definitely nothing less!

Next year they will decorate the house again, and the following year the garden

6
6

will get a remake if it hasn't come up to scratch by then. What a frustrating business this must be for a creative designer alert to the possibilities of a site and sensible of need for a sound match between what is possible and what is felt desirable. How stultifying to design to such a brief; little wonder then that recipes are developed that are repeated and repeated and repeated.

What to look for then, whether travelling in person or via the media? It is hard to put my finger on exactly what it is to look for; I think the first thing I do is get an impression of a garden, or a part of a garden, and take in some of the detail (a camera is a great help in this). Next, a sounding board is indispensable, someone to bounce ideas around with. What do you think of this? How do you feel about these colours? What strikes you about these plants? That sort of analysis helps to garner information that acts as a springboard for other ideas, but be careful, a garrulous companion can be a distinct distraction to observant contemplation and thoughtful serenity. Before leaving, I like to have another look, alone, at the parts of the garden that most aroused my interest and, if possible, I like to speak with the maker of the garden. This isn't always possible and it doesn't always work out, but it can be a help. Finally, I always keep notes that are made when there is time for some reflection and before my impressions get scrambled by other recollected gardens. Give yourself time and trust your instincts.

Obviously if you are obliged to keep up with a group, and may very likely be 'doing' four or five gardens (Heaven, forbid more) it will be difficult to follow these dictums. Then comes a necessary steeling of the will and a determined focus on getting the most out of what could be a once-in-a-lifetime opportunity. Some reading will help here, so do some homework if you can before you begin to travel, and badger the guide for tour notes too, so you can read up on what is in store. Be prepared for the bare fact that some gardens will just be pleasant viewing; this is just as well as you are probably on holiday and may enjoy the relaxation a green and flowery interlude will allow. And be ready for the one or two that you have decided may have something for your scrapbook. In some gardens, tour groups are severely herded about by strict guides with all the skills of a sheep-dog mustering a wayward flock; it may be impossible to escape, but give it a try unless the Polizza are likely to be summoned to attend to any breakaways. A toilet stop may provide an opportunity to study more closely the things you want to see rather than hearing about the glories of the Rococo aviaries, now seriously in advanced decay. However, be sure not to miss the bus.

What can be learned from a large, somewhat tatter-demallion Renaissance villa garden somewhere outside Rome? Look about and take in the picture: massive old trees,

A simple collection of trained geraniums adorn the verandah of a farmhouse near Molong in New South Wales.

bulky overblown hedges, rough grass, tall columnar cypresses, crumbling stone balustrades, stairs, basins, statuary, urns, large empty terracotta pots, dripping fountains, pools, a mossy grotto, runnels, rivulets and brilliant sunshine. What impressions do these create? Overall the cool, dark shadows, varied greens and the bulky mass of the growth contrast vividly with the harsh light, and the garden as a place of refuge from the heat and from the workaday world emerges as the moving force at work on the senses here. The garden has a powerful, still strength that has the capacity to invigorate fatigued bodies and minds.

Clearly, few will be able to carry away the whole concept and recreate it elsewhere; gardens of this scale and splendour are simply not possible now. But there are details and ideas that can be carried forth and remembered; things not to be copied stone for stone, plant for plant, but used to trigger ideas that can be developed in our own gardens. At one level of perception specific items draw attention: the use of potted hardy flowers such as geraniums, calla lilies and cannas to enliven the mass of greenery at key focal points in the garden. Note also that such pots are clustered together, thus making feeding and watering convenient, and also observe that the plants themselves

are well adapted and easy to care for in warm, dry climates. Turning to other
components, see the variety of materials used to make hard paving — old bricks,
cobbles, gravels, stone steps, shell-grit, sands — and make particular note of how these
are made more interesting for being laid in patterns and designs that may also
incorporate broken pots, broken tiles,
recycled concrete slabs, shells and
coloured pebbles.

   Although water is a scarce
commodity, consider how many different
ways a small volume can be used; the
fountains drip rather than roar, the
rivulets and runnels are only centimetres
wide and shallow at that, pools are
intimate rather than lake-like, spouts
spurt slender columns of water and after
ascending heavenward plop back to earth
rather than splashing and spraying. The
garden beds are of the simplest shapes,
mostly squares, rectangles and circles and
outlined uniformly in box and while the
patterns are evident, they are blurred
somewhat by the lumps and bumps of
age. All this contributes to the deep
repose of the garden that is further
enhanced by perceptions at another level
of awareness: the composition is
harmonious in its parts, the whole is
congruent with the climate and general
conditions of the place; the elements are
restrained, the colours refined and there
is an air of privacy and respite.

Drought-tolerant

   Let's take a magic carpet ride to California, making a landfall at Rancho del Sol,
home of Mrs Larry X. Biggerman VI. Our magic carpet comes to rest in a quiet leafy
street outside a pink-washed house with a walled courtyard and garage doors facing
the pavement.

Echeveria

secunda

6

9

Without going inside the garden walls, there is an immediate sense of drama about the garden; the skyline is punctuated with the forms of several kinds of palm tree, the plain walls of the forecourt throw into silhouette the trunks and branches of several columnar cacti and a dragon's blood tree (*Dracaena draco*). Inside the gate the courtyard is revealed as a simple patio. A small burbling fountain, a table, some chairs and several clusters of potted plants are all it contains. Vibrant pink and red bougainvilleas clothe the walls; shade is borrowed from the street trees and from trees planted outside the patio walls. Through wrought-iron gates other greenery hints at gardens beyond. A narrow side garden paved with fine, loose pebbles and planted with citrus and avocado trees backed with a high screen of star jasmine (*Trachelospermum jasminoides*) directs our way to a narrow opening between almost tropical growth of large, dark green leaves and opens onto a broad stone pavement under a pergola, vine covered and set with garden lounges. In the deep shade a hammock slung between two poles. Beyond the darkness, bright sunlight spotlights a sparkling swimming pool and beyond that a roofless colonnade of square, flat-topped pillars set against distant palms, eucalypts and loquat trees that close the garden. There are hints at Roman or Spanish origins, but no Old World garden ever was quite like this; the juxtaposition of the pool and the pillars is novel, and strictly a New World construction. Looking about more closely, we are aware of camellias potted in large Chinese tubs, tree ferns too, and hanging pots of orchids, leaf cactus, bromeliads and fuchsias. Suddenly the stillness is broken as hundreds of hidden jets spray water until everything is drenched. Thanks a lot, Mrs Biggerman.

What stands out in this, and many other California gardens, is the immense variety of plants and trees used and the intense use of flowering plants of all kinds. As we learned, there is also a great reliance on irrigation and technology to keep up the show.

Our impressions may well be those of massed colour, exotic foliage and bold forms; the structure less strongly emphasised than the images and impact of a series of enclosed spaces luxuriantly planted. Perhaps thoughts of a paradise on earth may strike the imagination. The scale is more intimate and domestic, suburban noise and the sight of roof lines and other houses intrudes somewhat on the perfection of the vision. The detail, busy and colourful, strikes a restless note. Concentrated might be a term to sum up the whole.

Magic carpet travel is all very well, but there are real gardens from which ideas can be gleaned too, and not necessarily just those in climates that are similar to our own. Visiting gardens in England is a very popular activity for tourists from everywhere.

The first delight is almost childlike at seeing flowers we can only dream about growing and at visiting gardens that are icons for good gardening. Then perhaps there may be a little disappointment that the gardens we see are not quite as perfect as the same gardens pictured in our well-thumbed books and magazines — there may be a few weedy corners, a few bare patches, the timing of much admired plant combinations and colour schemes may not align with our schedule. Then we have to deal with the crowds of people dawdling and jostling right in the middle of the famous vista, hurrying across allees and hovering in archways, and generally getting in the way.

So what? Having come a long way to see the place, never go away disappointed; even if it is pouring with rain, or if the day chosen for the visit is also chosen by five thousand others, there are many things that can be seen and remembered. It all depends on how you look at it.

To Hidcote then. The day is sunny and clear and even though it is just past opening time the car park proper is filled with cars and a few coaches, and the farm gate to the field beyond has been opened to take care of the overflow. The entrance is crowded but at least there are no queues. Once inside, just how many people are visiting becomes dishearteningly apparent. They are everywhere. A blue funk threatens but should be kept at bay; even the orchard and vegetable garden are thick with bodies. And as for the Stilt Garden, Theatre Lawn, Bathing Pool and Old Garden … just impossible. Perhaps taking tea and cake would give the crowds time to disperse? Not so, there seems to be no diminution of the throng. Maybe waiting until there is a gap in the crowd when the highlights of the garden's design can be seen for a fleeting moment in solitude. No such luck!

It does seem a problem does it not? How then to make the best of it? The best course of action is not to expect to see the garden from the carefully considered vantage points that the designer had in mind, but to attend more carefully to other features. Everyone who comes to Hidcote Bartrim Manor must surely come with prior knowledge of the glorious suite of garden rooms that unfolds as progress is made around the place. Pictured in almost every glossy house and garden magazine, the focused vistas and enclosed spaces are shown so perfectly without the intrusion of the human form that we can 'see' these parts of the garden at any time just by opening a book. What cannot be enjoyed so readily are the insights off-centre from the famous, and commonplace views of the garden. By looking for these it is quite easy to avoid the visual interference of a half a dozen bodies and it is very easy to appreciate that there is much more to Major Johnston's creation than a few well chosen focal points, an allee

7
1

and some handsome enclosed spaces. It is also possible to take good photographs 'off-centre', and if you're quick, without unwanted humans in view.

By adopting such a strategy, even the most crowded gardens such as Sissinghurst Castle can be visited with a guarantee of happy memories. And do not miss out strolling the well-known walks and being part of the admiring crowd doting over familiar plant

associations or adoring the great set pieces of plantsmanship; or in the case of Sissinghurst, jostling up those incredibly confined steps to the tower rooftop — enjoy the view as well and be part of the crowd. But reserve for yourself some quiet corners of the gardens, perhaps unseen by others hurrying by to get through and back on the bus. Carry these images home with you.

With this in mind let us turn to a few other gardens in England where the exposure to preconceived perfection is somewhat less, but the crowds just as daunting, and see what can be seen.

Denmans, near Fontwell in Sussex, is a garden I like to visit; I've only been there twice, but each time I have come away with a few ideas about plants to try and planting schemes to plot. It is not so big as many gardens that open on a regular basis so the ideas seem somehow less daunting than those on show in some other display gardens where full-time

Spectacular Geranium maderense

professional help is on tap. Coming from a place where the soil is lean and thinly laid upon the rocky subsoil, I have always used mulches of organic matter as freely as my purse allows, but have eschewed as unwise any thought of using hard inorganic mulches such as scoria and tumbled, broken bricks. At Denmans, lavish use is made of a deep mulch of small, water-worn, pea gravel and the plants thrive in it. My first reaction was to suppress the idea as one unsuited to my garden. After all, with the need to dig and

delve the gravel would surely contaminate what precious soil I already had and so further impoverish my gardening. Before my second visit I was confronted with further evidence on the value of mulching with stones and gravel. Christopher Lloyd has written several times in books and articles for *Country Life* about the way in which many plants self-sow and grow most prolifically, not in the garden beds we so carefully prepare for them, but in the edges of gravelled paths and drives, and between the cracks of paving stones and dry-stone walls. Now there is a man to sit up and take note of; at least I always find him so and he's right again (I've just remembered a self-sown but flagging plant of *Antirrhinum hispanicum* that needs a drink) about how these accidents of nature often produce results at least as good, and often better than the things we plan. My own observations on home ground convince me that there is something to be said for mulching with gravels. Seedlings of the wild cyclamen and all manner of perennials frequently appear in the gravel paths and driveways. Sometimes these are seedlings of plants long since departed the planned and maintained parts of the garden. Seedlings of *Asarina procumbens* volunteered years after the original plants died, appearing in an unlikely mix of gravel and bone-dry pine needle fragments. And welcome they were

Travelling with ideas—the Royal Pavilion at Brighton provides a striking counterpoint to garden visits in England and may spark ideas towards bolder, brighter gardens.

7

3

too, both this and the *Antirrhinum* are delightful snapdragons from Spain with greyish green trailing foliage and stems and creamy white flowers. Nearby I am trying to encourage *Nepeta tuberosa* to settle in among the chippings too. A decent depth of gravel would help and I am working on that. Once that is in place I can test my convictions more extensively.

Returning to Denmans the second time did not involve a breezy trip in a Citroen 2CV that enabled the first, but it did demonstrate clearly the value of Mediterranean plants and others from climates where the summers are sun-baked and dry, and it did show that such plants can make rich, bold designs provided conditions are right. Travel on the lookout for inspiration from which to spark fresh ideas should include a visit to Denmans. Other gardens with this focus in England are few; Beth Chatto's garden and nursery at White Barn House just outside Colchester in East Anglia is exceptional, but getting hold of some of the plants outside England could be a frustrating headache unless seed could be obtained and raised. The delay would be worth the wait if it were to give rise to a garden as exciting as this one. My last garden would be that made by Derek Jarman at Prospect Cottage on the shingle at Dungeness. For imaginative use of wild plants and tough perennials in very difficult circumstances, this would be hard to beat. And it is beautiful too. I dare say there is ample rain, more than that enjoyed by us visitors in our own gardens at home, but the pure shingle on which the garden is made would give instantaneous drainage that would render the garden 'dry'. Mr Jarman grew the native sea kale (*Crambe maritima*) to frothy perfection (and much more besides). My own attempts with this not-quite-a-vegetable-but-nor-yet-a-flower have failed twice, but I will keep trying; it should do well here on a scrumbly rubbly patch — half shale, half dirt. I have managed the sea hollies, *Eryngium maritimum* and *Eryngium campestre*, quite well and I want the kale to complement the two. More grit is what I need. Plants with deep-reaching, fleshy roots such as these two genera and artichokes (*Cynara cardunculus*) are reliable performers to which Mr Jarman has added many other plants equipped to deal with the salty and windy conditions. Waxy foliage, covered with hairs does the trick, quickly recovering from damage when supported by a stout root system. These characteristics of plant growth should be a guide to selecting plants not only for seaside gardens, but also those that grow where summer is hot and dry.

I think visiting Mr Jarman's garden must be a bookish expedition rather than the travelling kind. I'm not certain if the garden is ever open to visitors, but you can certainly read about it and see its charismatic mood captured in his book *Derek Jarman's Garden.*

7
4

I have travelled little in France and not at all in South Africa, so my impressions of the gardens there that might suddenly turn on the lights of inspiration in our mind are those gained from books and magazines and by talking to people. It would be unhelpful to my readers to draw on this meagre information to concoct any but the most elementary commentary on what might be learned from gardens in those places.

My first notion is that many old gardens in the Cape and in Provence (and possibly elsewhere in the south of France where turf won't grow) make good use of fine gravel and sand as a replacement for grass. I am thinking in particular of the sandy forecourts of *bastides* and *mas*, shaded by spreading plane trees where *petanque* or *boule* is played. These areas often seem to be set with tables and chairs too, showing that gravel and sand, though hard surfaces, are not necessarily a great discomfort to outdoor living and recreation. Lawns, lush and green, are not needed; fine gravel or sand raked or rolled makes an equally comfortable, even and serviceable surface.

The second notion I have is that a considerable number of the older homes in both countries make great use of big trees planted nearer to the house than modern building consultants would advise. I may be on shaky ground here, but I sometimes wonder if there is not as much myth as fact in the contemporary view that house foundations and trees are incompatible. In all of the Old World countries I have visited, people are happy to have large, mature trees to shade their house walls and create outdoor living areas just outside the door. These people take the view, sensibly from my perspective, that if the foundations need to be repaired every 100 years or so it is well worth the cost to enjoy the amenity the trees provide. Are those of us who live in the New World yet to come to this sensible and environmentally friendly solution? As it is, the only answer our building consultants can come up with to deal with the discomforts of sun-baked houses is to install ever-larger airconditioning units; an answer that is surely not friendly to the emissions-choked environment nor to the neighbours who must put up with the roaring noise of machinery all day and night.

Is it not a little surprising in these days of great engineering and technological skill that house foundations are such fragile things? That power utilities want us to consume ever more power, even with environmentally friendly star ratings, is hardly a puzzle. Could there be a conspiracy against 'real' trees, that is trees that grow more than three metres tall? The proposition that any problems induced by technology can be addressed with more technology seems a self-perpetuating conundrum. A step towards simpler solutions seems a likely avenue of investigation. Planting real trees might just be part of the answer — and not just for more comfortable houses.

7
5

A third impression arising from my recollected reading and looking is that besides acting as a place for recreation, and as a means of keeping homes tolerably cool in hot weather, these two features – sanded forecourts and great trees — combined to provide a useful extension to the living (and working) space of the house.

From my own childhood I can recall the newly arrived postwar migrants from southern Europe who bought up market gardening land around where I lived. Unable to enjoy the shade and shelter of big trees by their back doors, under which to chat, prepare food, eat and drink, and play bowls and cards, they quickly planted grape vines and constructed high trellises for them to grow over, thus continuing the 'best practice' that they knew for counteracting the heat of a protracted summer. These utilitarian pergolas provided an expedient replacement and doubled as a source of fruit for winemaking —

PREVIOUS PAGE:
(top) A tree-
shaded terrace
surrounded by
garden makes
for relaxed
outdoor living
in outback
Australia.
(bottom)
Making the
most of
borrowed
scenery is the
view from a
garden deck at
Pebble Beach
in California.
LEFT: Sheltered
in a natural
grove of coast
live oaks
(Quercus
agrifolia) at
Carmel Heights
in California
this living
space has been
designed to
prevent
damage to the
stand of
mature trees.

another excellent tradition in warm, dry climates. We have been conditioned to believe that we need large areas of smooth, immaculate and shaved grass to take our leisure outdoors. Some of our neighbours have shown us that this is not so; that there are affordable, practical alternatives. This multicultural spin-off bears further exploration and development as a design idea well suited to the climates where we live.

7

7

Now quite possibly there are those who think this idea has been fully explored and developed to the limit with technological adaptations and inventions which have resulted in metal and polycarbon constructions that reproduce the shade without the trees, without the fallen leaves and with the advantages of shade control through slats which open or close automatically via connected light sensors. In all probability temperature control is also achieved with gas heaters and evaporative coolers, and no doubt there is a heated spa bath that turns itself on 35 minutes before anyone arrives home from work! Somehow it all seems to have gone awry. The effortless complexities enabled by technology seem to have overtaken the simplicity of the idea. What is evident is that the original idea may be overdue for a revisit to review present 'improvements'. Travelling with ideas will enable such comparisons to be made.

One thing about travelling with ideas that never ceases to give me infinite pleasure is the way in which ideas suddenly arise in quite unexpected and unlikely places. Chains of associations sometimes bind our ideas into rather rigid and limited confines and getting free seems to be as much, or more a matter of chance than a result of planning. One of the most liberating experiences I have had was a chance visit to the Royal Pavilion at Brighton. In the middle of a very carefully planned trip during which time I saw many of the great English gardens, all my preconceptions were swept aside by a few hours spent indoors in a once-royal beach shack. Well intentioned friends had planned a day for me in the company of a landscape designer and set me up to expect a pleasant day chatting about 'business' and seeing some completed commissions. It didn't work out that way at all. No sooner had we got in the car and waved goodbye to my hosts than my new acquaintance declared that seeing yet more gardens would probably be a crashing bore so we would take a trip to Brighton instead, and see what the day produced. And that is what we did. Now it is probably being too glib to describe the Royal Pavilion as a beach shack. It is a most remarkable building, but it was intended only as a casual weekender for George IV as Prince of Wales; a place of light-hearted escape from the strictures of court etiquette. As such it was not meant to be a piece of serious architecture such as palaces are; it was just a *bon-bon*. But what a revelation it is; a place of Indian fantasy and Chinese magic and brilliant Oriental colour. Set against all the great Neo-Classical country houses — their exquisite (and pale) French decor and their Arcadian parklands — this one house sets all our ideas about the very essence of English attitudes towards colour and decoration atumble. Having had several weeks of pastel borders gently grading from one colour harmony to another it was electrifying to suddenly realise the piquancy that can be achieved by doing something wildly different, doing it well with good materials and doing it convincingly from beginning to end. The dawning of this idea in my mind convinced me of the value of not copying what everyone else is doing; I'm no great decorator but as a gardener I could understand the implications for my handiwork.

Although there are many experiences which influence the way we change from tourists to travellers, I think perhaps this last is the one from which we can learn most. Being open to the possibilities offered by chance and being willing to depart from the track we have chosen to beat. Yes, there are many lovely gardens around the world for us to visit, and from which we may learn, not to copy but to spark ideas. The generation of ideas that lead to new directions in our gardens can be an exciting and creative experience for all who garden with passion. The sense of discovery and revelation — the impetus to move forward — heightened by the appearance every so often of another kind of garden, adds that certain *frisson* to our appreciation.

E N C L O S E D   B E H I N D
walls

One of the most striking differences between gardens in the Old World and the New, at least as far as gardens in warm, dry climates go, are the apparently opposite attitudes towards the deliberate enclosure of gardens.

In Spain and Italy, gardens seem mostly to exist behind high walls; their existence hinted at only by trees towering above the walls or by trails of climbing plants sprawling over them. Entered only at the invitation of the owner they are intensely private places. Whether the walls are made of elegantly dressed stone, rubble plastered smooth or ancient bricks, they have tremendous possibilities for garden making.

Strolling down a street in some ancient southern European town as it winds along the side of a hill, with corners and bends so sharp cars cannot pass without much tooting, advancing and backing, it is quite easy to understand that they were never

PREVIOUS PAGES:

(p. 80) A view

into an

enclosed

garden at

White

Windows,

Hampshire—

how much

more

appropriate

to warm dry

climates is the

idea of

enclosure?

(p. 81) Tulipa

sylvestris *from*

southern Italy,

Sardinia and

Sicily

meant to carry motor traffic. Well-worn cobbles, kerb stones and gutters and the foundations of walls and house all merge into each other in an almost organic growth, rutted and pocked with age. What made those marks? How long have these walls and roads existed? What have they seen? Quite possibly a flock of Medieval nuns could canter around the next corner, harness bells a-jingle and singing of their pilgrimage to Compostella; or maybe a squad of Roman soldiers will be resting in the black shadows under the trees ahead. Walls and pavements are a real link with a past we mostly never knew; we live in places where walls are few, frowned on and forbidden by many modern 'open' communities, and yet there is an immediate response to them. It is a quiet response almost latent; the sight of them stirs us with easy, comfortable feelings. We may not be able to enter through any of the gates shut against the outsiders in the street, but we sense and know the power of walls that since ancient times have enclosed and sheltered our lives against harsh environments and unfriendly strangers.

Settlers to the New World also made walls and while we may fancifully guess at the reasons for the existence of old European walls, the causes for walls being erected by colonials were largely to do with keeping valuable cattle, horses and sheep from roaming too far, or to keep herds of livestock from eating precious vegetable and fruit gardens, and to act as a deterrent to marauding bands of natives. In a few places, kilometres of dry-stone walls enclose fields and paddocks; still standing after a hundred years and more, they are powerful memorials to the unseen hands of children and women who gathered the stones from the fields while their menfolk slowly constructed the walls to traditional patterns brought from distant homelands. One way and another, protection and defence were what most early walls in Australia, California and the Cape were about.

It is very heartening to see how greatly these old walls are becoming valued nowadays. It was only a few years ago that old walls in need of repair were bulldozed and 'mined' for their stone, and quite often used for filling on building sites. Unless conserved by protection orders at heritage sites, their future seemed short and bleak. How this has changed; not only are old walls now incorporated in many new development plans, but new ones are made using the old skills; dry-stone walling is taught in technical colleges and it has taken on a role as a developing art form. New walls too, are being built on every hand; proper walls of stone, brick and rubble — solid and long-lasting; some new looking, yet others carefully distressed to appear old and still others created in a post-Modern version of architectural ruins just like the fake ruins built as follies and eye-catchers in old European landscape gardens. It is all very encouraging.

There will be those who scoff at such enthusiasm; first those who still want to maintain a wide-open, on-show approach to the places where we live; second will be those technophiles who want to do it all with scanners and detectors and rays and beams, and I dare say there will be yet others who will protest that we are turning in on ourselves and developing a fortress mentality. Perhaps there is something to be said in support of all these points of view. I am just a gardener; I move daily in society and am not insensitive to the intrusive and aggressive nature of some aspects of our culture. But in making a garden and wishing for a wall or two, I do not seek to avoid those who work and live around me; I merely wish to create a sense of enclosure, a feeling of intimacy and a suggestion of privacy. And I am content to observe that boundaries do exist and are marked. My concern is that these limits to access so often find expression in the ugliest of mediums: the corrugated iron fence, the galvanised chain-link fence and the marginally better fibro-cement fencing panels. All of them are incredibly ugly and are difficult to disguise; as a background to a garden they are an eyesore. On the grounds of economy these things may be necessary, but they can never replace a wall. They just do not have the personality. No matter what is done to screen a tin fence it still glints and glistens from behind it's veil of greenery, glowering like some malevolent spectre.

What can I do but point to it? Walls have each their own history … presence … magic.

One of the most creative gardens I know has been made within the walls of a ruined jam factory. Do not imagine a vast range of derelict buildings. This was just a simple building, rectangular and half sunk into the side of a gentle hill slope, with three rooms. The roof and timbers disappeared years ago, as did the equipment, if there ever was any apart from simple cauldrons and a hearth. The building is partly open for about two-thirds of its out-facing wall, suggesting the possibility of long-gone doors. Now what remains gives three sunken 'rooms' with interconnecting doorways and the large openings outward into what has become a garden. The floors are paved in part with large cut and fitted slate slabs but some of these have been scavenged by others so there are large gaps in the floor. These have been used to plant all manner of hardy perennials — the garden gets no irrigation in summer. Outside the building other plants have been set close to the walls so that they can tumble over the walls, down into the interior garden rooms. A few simple, rustic branches trimmed of side growth and bark placed across some of the corners of the walls offer climbers and trailers scrambling room and the shadows thrown by their growth creates a little shade in the rooms beneath. It is all

FOLLOWING PAGE:
(p. 84) An old dry-stone wall made by early settlers at Glen Osmond in South Australia. The ivy is all that is needed to complement the lichen-covered leaves of slate (top). Large river-washed boulders piled up to make a boundary wall, Carmel Valley, California (bottom).

8
3

very charming and a delightful suntrap on clear winter days. Not everyone, of course, will be lucky enough to find such a happy ruin, but imagine the owner's pleasure at

making a garden in such a magical situation. Nasturtiums trail down the walls and cover parts of the floor while hollyhocks tower about high overhead. Ox-eye daisies (*Leucanthemum vulgare*) spangle the floor and colonise parts of the wall as do Kenilworth ivy (*Linaria cymbalaria*), *Sisyrinchium striatum* (syn. *Phaiophelps nigricans*) and blue-eyed grass (*Sisyrinchium bellum*) — which hasn't changed its name, yet! Earlier there would have been jonquils, freesias, babianas and the mysterious dragon lily (*Dracunculus vulgaris*), but these have died down with the advent of early summer. A huge mound of 'Mme Gregoire Staechelin' smothers a pile of rubble and throws long, arching

canes partly over one corner of the building. It has no voluptuous pink roses at this time, but is covered with a fine crop of large, pale-green hips. It takes care of itself and always has done. Everything is self-sowing or self-sufficient so maintaining the 'ruined' aura, and allowing the owner to pursue a career as an artist in an inspirational atmosphere.

Aside from an intrinsic aura of ancient wellbeing, walls also give gardeners many opportunities to use them to advantage. Should a garden be blessed with boundary walls sufficiently high to screen the garden within from outside, there will be opportunities to play hide-and-seek, to conceal or reveal particular features of the landscape in the outside world. A doorway with a grille in the door could allow a partial glimpse into a field. A similar doorway giving into a street

PREVIOUS PAGE:

(p. 85)

*A gravelled
entrance court
surrounded by
high garden
walls and
simply
decorated with
large
terracotta pots
at La Bonne
Maison, France
(top).*

*No decoration
is needed to
add to the
strength of this
colonial
Spanish-
American wall
in the Schlegel
garden
(bottom).*

could allow passers-by a tantalising view of greenery and flowers. Visual contrasts between the strength of the work and the delicacy or boldness of foliage could be developed by sensitive planting. Careful selection of climbing plants could enhance the colour of the masonry or paint-washed wall surface. Grey stone walls could be enlivened with the bold orange-red trumpets of *Campsis grandiflora* or the rich yellow flowers of *Macfadyena unguiscati;* equally effective would be *Campsis x tagliabuana* 'Mme Galen' (red) or *Campsis radicans* 'Flava'. Those with a bold approach to colour could choose the black-flowered coral pea, *Kennedia nigricans*. An altogether cooler colour scheme could be built around the large blue trumpets of *Thunbergia grandiflora* or the lilac stars of *Petrea volubilis*. These colours would look just as telling set against almost any other coloured stone.

Brick walls would require a degree more care and, in my view look best when the greenery of covering vines is the major colour note. I would be inclined towards planting *Vitis coignetiae*, *Vitis vinifera* 'Purpurea' or *Vitis amurensis*. It is not so easy to match coloured flowers sympathetically to the varied rusty, orange and mottled brown shades of brickwork, so if colour harmonies are important, white or cream flowered vines may be the best choice rather than risking a visual migraine. The likes of *Ipomoea alba* (syn. *Calonyction aculeatum*), *Mandevilla laxa*, *Pandorea jasminoides* 'Alba', *Pandorea pandorana* 'Alba' and *Trachelospermum jasminoides* would all fit the bill elegantly. The dusky rose-pink flowers of *Tecomanthe venusta* could be just right to complement the range of tones found in bricks while the brilliant scarlet stars and deep green leaves of *Passiflora coccinea* could be an attraction in a bold colour scheme. Ivies also go well with brickwork as their coverage tends to be like a blanket thrown over a wall, making a solid sheet of colour with no intrusive undercolour reds showing through. I have a soft spot for the clean-cut, bold, golden variegation of the Algerian ivy, *Hedera colchica* 'Dentata Variegata', but there are plenty of other good candidates to choose from. How about the all-yellow leaves of *Hedera helix* 'Buttercup' or the plain green shovel-shaped leaves of *Hedera helix* 'Deltoidea', or another favourite of mine, *Hedera canariensis* 'Albo-maculata' with leaves so heavily variegated that they appear white with a covering of fine dark-green spots. It is very slow to get established, but it is so spectacular in a shaded nook at the base of a wall. A last choice would be another form of the reliable Canary Island ivy, *Hedera canariensis* 'Paddy's Pride', in which the large dark green leaves have a central blotch of golden yellow, not a knock-out variegation but a subtle touch of colour that adds distinction to a valuable climber for warm, dry climates.

I realise as I write just how restrained my vision is; such gentle Anglo-European ideas. Let us spread our wings a bit and think more widely. My first thoughts turn to a house not far from where I live; there is a high, cement-rendered wall with high gates and the piers are capped with classical Roman statues — a rare hybrid of naive art and multiculturalism. At one side the wall is painted a dark, dull Roman red — the colour of wine — while another side presents a pale blue facade to the street. Now there is a wall that cries out for some colourful vine to heighten the drama. That claret red calls for something really powerful; I think an even stronger, more brilliant wine colour would be up to the colour of the wall. And something that would produce sheets of pure colour; *Bougainvillea x* 'Carmencita' (syn. 'Klong Fire') would be splendid. This is a compact-growing double-flowered form. Larger growing and single flowered *B. x* 'Scarlett O'Hara' could also find a place in such a scheme. A shade or two towards a vibrant deep pink is *Distictis buccinatoria* — the Mexican blood flower; it would look good too, set in contrast to the burgundy-coloured background. To set things off with a real sparkle, I would seed the crack between the base of the wall and the tar-macadam pavement with purple-flowered *Verbena rigida* and *V. bonariensis* and with the bronze-leaved form of fennel, *Foeniculum communis*. If I could contrive it, a bronze-leaved cordyline (*Cordyline australis* 'Purpurea') would raise a feathery top above the wall. The self-sown weedy fennel and verbenas could continue around the corner to the pale blue facade of the wall. Here I could imagine a curtain of *Ipomoea palmata* with its large lavender trumpets, or the diminutive but prolific purple thimbles of *Asarina barclaiana* (syn. *Maurandia barclaiana*). It might be possible to persuade *Cobea scandens* to scramble up and over the wall too. Its purple cup and saucer flowers would look intresting scattered among the smaller thimble flowers of the twining snapdragon. On a purely pragmatic note, such as I suspect would appeal to the owners of the wall, the banana passionfruit, *Passiflora mollissima*, would make such a wall home and look good to boot.

Well, there is a selection of moderate climbers suited to growing over garden walls in medium-sized gardens. There has been no mention of some old stalwarts such as climbing fig (*Ficus pumila*) and the chalice vine (*Solandra maxima*) because I know they grow very large and need much attention to keep under control in gardens where they cannot be allowed to romp away freely into the treetops; like wisterias, they can easily get out of hand. Nor has there been any mention of the numerous and very beautiful forms of *Bomarea* spp. — the climbing alstromerias; they are moderate in growth but are not commonly seen in nurseries or gardens. They deserve wider use, but also need watering over the hot, dry months. Perhaps they could become a focus of interest for

87

Mission San Carlos Borromeo de Carmelo—the large quadrangle between the church and mission buildings is simply planted with a rich selection of flowering drought-tolerant plants, Carmel, California.

those who enjoy trying new things from seed. Jim and Jenny Archibald often list numerous species in their seed list (see page 197). One larger-growing climber that is worth trying is the Burmese honeysuckle, *Lonicera hildebrandiana*, which has very large, well-scented flowers that open pale cream and develop deep golden yellow shades as each flower matures. It is tolerant of light frosts once it has established a woody framework of growth.

Let us now return to considering walls.

It is all very well wishing for walls, but as few of us live in ancient cities most will have to make do with whatever can be contrived. At least now that urban infill is creating a denser pattern of housing, the need for walls has become legitimate, and that is a step or two in the right direction. Open-plan living in houses open to view is fine if the neighbours are discreet, or perambulate far enough away to prevent them having a bird's eye peek at everything going on indoors, but once houses and foot traffic are close, some privacy is required. The most common walls seem to be modelled on some sort of Victorian-Edwardian pastiche; tall square piers regularly spaced with a solid infill of single-course brickwork, the whole finished with render and mouldings that suggest panels and a squat pyramidal finial. Perhaps there are inset panels of reproduction cast-iron lace (in aluminium). A similar model, without the imitation mouldings and finial, is regurgitated for more modern homes. In each case they are uniformly two metres tall, and they are all in desperate need of plants to soften their

hard, fresh edges and to add some colour to relieve the boredom of endless mock

sandstone or tumbled bricks. Wouldn't it be something if a few individuals could

persuade the craftsmen employed on such massive constructions to rusticate their work

with a few uneven lumps and bumps, or to create some carefully distressed corners and

edges to break down the relentless perfection? A picture framer that I know swears

motor-bike drive-chains are ideal implements for this purpose. The work of antiquing a wall can be taken further with a wash of diluted yoghurt or a water-based lime wash used in two or three slightly different shades to enhance the shadows cast by mouldings and generate some instant grime. Any more and I will be giving away trade secrets — and that would never do, would it?

Other walls are possible and are only limited by the materials available and the skills necessary for solid construction. One wall that stays in my mind's eye is one I saw in the Carmel Valley in California. It was in fact rather old, having been made as a boundary marker for one of the original Spanish-Mexican ranchos established there before California became part of the United States. The wall is made of large, rounded river rocks, not pebble or cobble size, nor yet boulders, but about canonball size. Light enough to lift readily but too heavy to be easily dislodged by animals or humans. These have been piled up without any mortar so the wall is considerably wider at its base than at the apex. I imagine that on a ranch of many thousands of hectares a few square metres taken up by the wall wouldn't have been a consideration. Once the sole built feature in a remote corner of the ranch, the wall now sits in a leafy glade surrounded by a cluster of homes; in all probability parts of it have been rebuilt over the years and such is the impact this silent monument has that it has never been 'improved' with cement or modernised. Running straight and true for hundreds of metres, the wall has the presence that many modern sculptors wish could be imbued by their works — and some of them are not that dissimilar! A wall of this kind that has grown out of its setting, built from stones gathered on the spot, needs no further adornment but the trees that shade it and the dry yellow grass that surrounds it. In parts the gardens of the homes around approach it, yet the bright annuals and perennials hardly touch the strength of its solid dark grey hues; it is almost as if the stones soak up the colours. Elaine and Mark Schlegel, professional landscapers in whose garden the wall runs for most of its length, recognise the power of the simple construction and wisely let it speak for itself. Gathering such stones may or may not be possible today, according to the environmental laws in force, but given the long-term purpose this wall has served it seems likely its makers could be forgiven for disturbing the creek bed from which the stones were collected. A frivolous, throw-away construction would be unforgivable, but to my way of thinking this is a legitimate use of a natural resource.

I know another wall that could hardly be a greater contrast. Made of old building rubble, broken bricks and reinforced with wrecked bicycles and other domestic flotsam, it has been rendered with rough-cast cement bagged off smooth and painted a vivid cobalt blue. A blue so brilliant that traffic slows when passing by. There is no coping and there are no piers so the wall has no shadows playing over its surface. It is just a pure, piercing deep blue. Simple and stunning.

In towns and villages where a classical town white-scape commands conformity such a wall may not be possible, though even in pristine, picture-perfect Thira on Santorini there are strong touches of colour here and there. A good many plain walls, unadorned even by a lick of colour, could easily be converted at a stroke, well, at a few strokes, to a focal point of which much can be made by an enterprising garden maker. Having already discussed a dark red wall and now a deep blue one, there are other strong bold colours that could also be used. Burnt sienna is a colour well-known from childhood paint boxes that would be one possibility, and there is also a range of ochres that would add further strong browns to the list. Not any greens I think, they are too close to the colours of plants to provide that essential, breath-taking difference; unless perhaps one of the stark acid greens that tends towards yellow that might work well with plants that have red or purple foliage. Some of the hot, fluorescent Caribbean pinks, oranges and blues could work too, but being such obviously man-made, chemical colours they may need a setting among rich tropical greenery to be effective. The colours of the Mediterranean seem to be tied to the colours of earth and sky rather than the plumage of tropical birds and flowers. If a brightly coloured wall seems right for a particular piece of a garden design the opportunity presents itself for some experimentation, so there is no need to feel tied to my responses to colour in the environment.

To make use of such colour and the absolute simplicity of the wall is not a problem. Having decided to have, say, a rich brown wall of burnt sienna, it would be a backward step to hide it behind the drapery of a climber. Why not use it as a stage setting for some spectacular foreground plants? The idea would be to choose a few, very few, plants that have their own boldness and power; plants with strong silhouettes and that quality of mass that will enable them to counterbalance the weight of the wall in the scene. In artists' terms what I am suggesting is that a restricted palette of colour and form would be ideal in this situation. What would suit? Something with yellow, orange or red flowers I would suggest. And what sort of plants? Aloes appeal to me for this purpose; the tree forms have wonderful shapes and very strong architectural forms; some species have leaves that develop bronze tones that would add to the picture being composed and within the whole family there is a wide range of plants that give plenty of scope for choice and variety. Sadly, aloes have been much overlooked in recent years

ABOVE: *The
patio within
the walls of
the Presidio,
Old Monterey,
California.*
RIGHT: *A high,
white-washed
fence topped
with a rustic
pergola, San
Juan Bautista,
California.*

and the available range has shrunk to a
fraction of that once widely grown by
gardeners in temperate climates so
finding suitable plants could be a chase
through all kinds of backyard and mail
order nurseries specialising in succulent
plants. It will be interesting even though
time-consuming, and it will give support
to a group of growers who do try to
maintain a wide range of stock. For the
wall under consideration I would try to
locate plants of *Aloe angelica* which is a
tree-form aloe with bronze leaves and
candelabras of tubular, yellow flowers.
Other tree-like possibilities could be *Aloe
dolomitica, Aloe bainesii, Aloe ferox, Aloe
marlothii* or *Aloe africana*. To balance the

composition I would seek a large plant of *Aloe plicatilis*, the book-leaf aloe. This is a compact, shrubby form of aloe which produces small spikes of coral-coloured flowers in winter; it is more freely available than many other forms and even large multi-branched cuttings can be easily rooted in dry sand. By this means, quite large, landscape-sized plants can be acquired within a few months of being severed from a parent plant.

To complete the simple planting, a low-growing species could be included such as *Aloe gariepensis, Aloe chabaudii, Aloe ammophila* or *Aloe cryptopoda*. Tall growing euphorbias such as *Euphorbia ingens, Euphorbia cooperii* or *Euphorbia grandicornis* would also be excellent choices and would enable a more varied display of plant forms. Where heavy frosts or severe hail storms are prevalent, aloes and euphorbias cannot be expected to grow well so other, less hard-edged compositions may need to be substituted. I would suggest yuccas as a reasonable replacement genus. Completely different in outline and just as telling would be *Opuntia robusta*, one of the tree-sized prickly pears with large circular silvery leaf pads. It offers the advantage of attractive yellow flowers and masses of dark red fruits somewhat larger than golf-balls (which are edible, though not as tasty as other species of the genus). There are many prickly pears, or tunas grown in the climatic regions in which we make gardens, but these are grown primarily for their fruit; their appearance and habits of growth are rarely of concern to those who grow them. In this case appearance is important, so it is worth the trouble of obtaining a form superior to others. Other prickly pears with attractive pads, flowers and fruits are listed on pages 182-183.

Shadow patterns play on the walls and sanded courtyard in the Presidio at Old Monterey.

9
3

It is just as well to write here a few words about maintaining plants such as aloes, euphorbias and prickly pears so that their appearance is always smart. All too often these plants are allowed to retain the mass of dead leaves which accumulates over the years under the growing points. In view of the hard, sharp image we are endeavouring to create against the solid bulwark of a wall I suggest that careful removal of spent leaves is a worthwhile use of a gardener's time. Naturally, where plants with spiky leaves are concerned care must be taken to avoid injury to skin or eyes, and a check made that tetanus booster shots are up to date.

There remains one other sort of wall that is worth looking at, especially in those places where old walls are not possible. I am referring to that brand of modern architecture which achieves its impact by a kind of post-Industrial ruinism. In this the perfect geometry of a blank wall is disrupted by a gigantic fracture, through which an inner, and contrasting plain surface is revealed. This is cutting-edge stuff chaps! The impression is of a fractured archaeological remnant within which a new habitation has been built of black glass or some other stark and impenetrable medium. As a piece of drama it is at once mysterious and enigmatic. Has an atomic bomb dropped here or has an earthquake devastated this place? What happened here? What now happens inside? Since the architect has gone to such trouble to create such a carefully crafted piece of the Picturesque, any efforts to garden must add to the feeling of desolation rather than ameliorate it. My response would be that the impact of the shattered concrete edges of the cleft which has been rent through the heart of the building could be enhanced with simple, uncomplicated plants such as might regenerate after some world-shattering event. A mix of grasses, a few almost weedy perennials and maybe a scrambling vine would probably be all that is needed. Trees, if any, would be limited to a colonising kind such as the tree of heaven (*Ailanthus altissima*) or if that is ruled out on account of its reputation as a thug in civilised gardens, perhaps an olive (*Olea europaea*), sweet bay (*Laurus nobilis*) or Russian olive (*Elaeagnus angustifolius*). For a vine I would not go past the hop (*Humulus lupus*) which is sufficiently wild-looking and free in its growth without there being any risk of it getting out of hand. It would need a few holding points to get it up the wall. These could be discreetly inserted without disturbing the singular ambience of the setting. As to the requisite grasses and perennials, I would go with one of the fountain grasses that does not seed readily — *Pennisetum alopecuroides* — and I would match it with my old pets *Verbena rigida* and *V. bonariensis*. For weedy variety I would add plants of blue and white wild chicory (*Cichorium intybus*) and either plain fennel (*Foeniculum vulgare*) or the giant fennel (*Ferula communis*).

Come to think of it, almost any simple combination of plants that constitute 'wild food' could be attractive, curious and suitable. For further fascinating reading search out Euell Gibbon's *Stalking the Wild Asparagus* Among those wild foods that come to mind are artichokes, all manner of herbs, mustard greens, garlic, kales, Jerusalem artichokes, salsify, scorzonera, lima bean, maybe even chokos (Christophine's) and yes, asparagus too.

Now, for someone who hasn't got a single metre of wall I think I've done a fair piece of work in setting my readers on track concerning how best to make the most of such a asset in a garden. But what if walls are not a possibility for you? They very well may still be a necessity for their qualities as providers of privacy and security, or for their usefulness as wind breaks and as the means of breaking up large garden spaces into more intimate and secluded areas; creating by their presence a sense of progress and suggesting movement through a garden by what they reveal and what may be hidden. All is not lost if garden walls are out of the question. Hedges can provide an almost-as-good answer, though their all over greenness rules out some of the more exciting possibilities for imaginative planting. And stylistically they all tend to be much of a muchness, pretty well full square and trimly kept. This is as it should be with hedges; they need to be trim and square to look their best. Forget hedges with curved surfaces unless you have trained as a tonsorial artist; keeping these smooth and evenly cut requires very steady hands and eyes, and a degree of patience granted to very few. As to 'ruined' hedges or some other sort of post-Modern style I am not sure how it could be done without a great deal of highly skilled topiary work, nor am I certain of what such a hedge might look like or if a hedge could be made that would retain its basic characteristics as a wind break, screen and security feature. Maybe there is a challenge there for some conceptual artist to get to work thinking about the idea?

When talking of hedges and gardens in Mediterranean climates it is critical to understand that such garden devices, while very worthwhile, are not without their disadvantages. Trimming aside, and what an aside that is, the root structures of plants that can be used for hedges in warm, dry climates are generally far-reaching and hungry for water and nutrients. This means that they must be very carefully placed, preferably with some barrier to their roots reaching other parts of the garden. A physical barrier could be sunk into the ground a metre and more deep in the hope of restraining the spread of hedge roots to other parts, or the hedge could be set at some distance to other garden parts by separating the two by a broad path or paved area. Another wise precaution against far-ranging roots is to organise for a separate

irrigation system for the hedge, thus encouraging its roots not to wander far and wide
in search of water.

Consideration also needs to be given to the kinds of plants best suited to
hedges in the climatic zones we are interested in. Many plants considered suitable for
hedges in other climates simply do not have the constitution to see them safely
through annual periods of heat and drought. Hedge plants which suddenly develop

dead bits are usually found to have suffered from drought, have lost vigour and become subject to attack by borers. As hedges these plants are a dead loss. Some species and garden clones of cypress (*Cupressus* spp.) are particularly prone to drought-induced dieback in situations where summer droughts are regular. As we do not wish to plant hedges which are overly water-dependent it is wise to observe such plants carefully in local gardens before purchasing them. It is one thing to water a hedge regularly until it is well established; another entirely to have to water it all its long life. It is just as bad to have to replace an unsatisfactory hedge two years or so after it has been planted.

Good choices for hedges in areas where summers are hot and dry are fairly restricted, not that this is necessarily such a huge disadvantage; it does create a sort of local unity and continuity in the landscape. Pragmatic locals in the areas where many of us are residents have in the past planted utilitarian hedges that are truly defensive and sometimes productive. Prickly pears (*Opuntia ficus-indica*) and tall, columnar forms of

ABOVE: *An allee of trees and a sanded walk make a fine spot for relaxing in the shade while screening and framing views to other parts of the garden at Hidcote Manor.*

LEFT: *A sunny patch of lawn for the grandchildren to play on sets the tone for relaxation in this elegant French garden.*

9
7

cacti such as *Cereus* spp. have been popular choices along with the impenetrable clumping rosettes of *Agave americana* and *Agave sisalana*. With their leaves armed along the edges with sharp, hooked thorns they are enough to deter anyone. But these are not perhaps the best hedges for home gardens; their place is around fields of vegetables and orchard groves where their armature is an appropriate discouragement to thieving.

Home gardeners will generally want something less dangerous and more able to provide adequate screening. Among the best are the common olive (*Olea europaea*) and the carob (*Ceratonia siliqua*) for they are evergreen, drought-tolerant and adaptable to a wide range of soils. They also respond well to clipping and make dense, compact growth right down to ground level. Furthermore, they require trimming only once a year and, so far as I have observed them, they do not die out in unbecoming patches. Rather slower is the holm oak (*Quercus ilex*), but also a very good choice where a hedge with some stature (three metres plus) is called for in the scheme of the garden. Remember that we are discussing the use of hedges as garden walls and so I have not gone into any consideration of the many plants that can be used as a means of making low dividing walls within a garden. Nor have I discussed 'fedges' an ugly term which some experts of the Royal Horticultural Society promote to describe the lax hedges such as those of shrub, rambling and climbing roses trained along posts and horizontal wires to make a screen. I am not opposed to new words, indeed bureaucrats among my readers will have observed that this book 'promotes a paradigm shift in domestic horticultural practice in a non-threatening ethos, seeking positive outcomes for change through collaborative support and pragmatic exemplars'. But I do not like 'fedges' as a new term for garden screens and I am struck dumb by the newly proposed term for perennial sub-shrubs: 'prubs'! Ye Gods!.

Other suitable choices for a substantial hedge could be the hedge thorn (*Carissa bispinosa*), the Natal plum (*Carissa macrocarpa*), silver berry (*Elaeagnus pungens*), *Elaeagnus x ebbingei*, *Escallonia bifida*, the lentisc (*Pistacia lentiscus*), the pomegranate (*Punica granatum*) and the firethorns (*Pyracantha angustifolia* and *Pyracantha coccinea*). As these have been chosen as good hedging plants I have not thought it necessary to go into detail about their flowers and fruits as these are very much of secondary importance to the purpose of hedge-making, however, those of the carissas and the pomegranate are edible.

Making low partitions with a garden may prove a vexing exercise for those keen to reproduce some sort of parterre as part of a garden. Competition for the available moisture between the hedging plants and the floral in-fill of such a garden would be intense and I think it most likely the hedge would win out, leaving the flowers always looking parched and tatty: not the desired effect at all. As it is not desirable to water heavily and frequently in the style of gardening we have in mind, a better strategy might be to consider a plainer version of the same idea wherein the flowers are omitted. The effect is of a patterned carpet of green, hence the French name *tapis vert*. This idea is well tried and will be found in many old gardens in southern Europe. If colour is wanted to highlight the scheme, let it take the form of annuals in large pots as the old gardens demonstrate. Given that summer should be the months during which our gardens and ourselves take a rest it may be an even better idea simply to have a garden of greens while the heat lasts.

Enclosed with high hedges that make walls of greenery and with a background of varied greens shown in relief against gravel and paving stones, surely the summer would seem cooler and we would be refreshed in readiness for garden work in the autumn.

A New

orchard

and Garden

'Art hath made her first Original out of Experience, which therefore is called The School-Mistress of Fools, because she teaches infallibly, and plainly, as drawing her knowledge out of the course of Nature, (which never fails in the general) by the senses, feelingly apprehending, and comparing (with the help of the Mind) the Works of Nature; and as in all other things natural, so especially in Trees.'

So begins William Lawson to 'all well-minded' folk in his preface to *A New Orchard & Garden*, published in 1618. It is a book I have in facsimile on my shelves and one I like to look at often. Once I thought to buy an original edition, but the copy offered turned out to be wormy and tattered; though it was charming I didn't want it enough to part with $500 so it failed to find the buyer that lurks not far beneath my skin.

PREVIOUS PAGES:

(p. 100) A
garden grove
of potted
lemon trees,
Villa
Torrigiani,
Tuscany,
(p. 101) Dietes x
'Orange Drops'

Why is it that the book stays with me on my shelves of working books? It stays because it explores some ideas about gardening which were new at the time of publishing, and which I have found to be worthwhile revisiting. Lawson was one of the earliest English advocates for 'scientific' methods of planting and tending orchards, and for the selection and propagation of improved varieties of fruit trees, particularly apples. His book had bound with it other small books on beekeeping and domestic gardening. This latter tract is titled *The Country House-wifes Garden for Herbs of Common use. Their Virtues, Seasons, Ornaments, Variety of Knots, Models for Trees, and Plots, for the best Ordering of Grounds and Walks.*

What I really like about this small book is the way it stimulated my thinking in directions that were new to me. What struck me was the way in which gardens in warm, dry climates could be ordered, an orchard form laid out on a grid and planted with the same or similar trees. Visual impact, shelter from the elements, overhead shade, utility if that were wanted, unity, strength of line, shadow movement — an idea which could be played around with in endless combinations of formality and informality, with flowers or without, as an essay in greens. The ideas seemed to run on and on.

Since being hit by this brainwave I have realised that the idea is much older than Lawson. Indeed, it goes back to the very beginnings of gardening in ancient Egypt. The idea is that of orchards as places that were adorned with flowering and perfumed plants, where people could relax and enjoy a few moments outdoors in the shade surrounded by bounty and beauty. Read any book about growing fruit trees and you will quickly discover what a chore it is taken to be. Every aspect of fruit-growing is descibed as work. Little wonder then that most of us have been put off by the whole deal and buy our Golden Delicious, Fuji and Granny Smith apples from a roadside stall or the greengrocer. As I gathered examples of the orchard as a garden from magazines and books, I also realised that the idea is one which is still widely practised, but not so much by pleasure gardeners as by small farm holders in southern and eastern Europe. For them, the wildflowers that grow in the turf beneath their groves of plum, almond, apricot, peach and olive trees are nothing more than a happy coincidence; something that may give their children pleasure in gathering, or something to feed the family goat. At the other end of society, there will be a few whose estate gardens include orchards where utility will almost certainly go hand in hand with beauty by combining trees and flowers deliberately. The balance will most likely favour the flowers over fruit; gnarled apple trunks will provide a living support for climbing roses and clematis; the ground beneath the Morello cherries will be carpeted with tulips, wallflowers, daisies and primroses. The transformation from production to decoration will be complete if the fruit-bearing trees are grubbed out and replaced with flowering kinds.

Pleasure gardeners who have bought houses attached to old orchards have a novel and entire setting in which to focus their creativity. An orchard is an environment in itself, a complete landscape that can be rejuvenated, revealed, enhanced or decorated, though what a shame to so alter it that it is no longer an orchard.

A block of subdivided land cut out of old orchard groves or market gardens could be soothed back into the established landscape by replanting the bones of the garden as an orchard; maybe even to the fine degree of realigning the new trees with the old tree rows, if they can be located. Even a block of land cut from native scrub could be planted as an orchard with obvious links back to the gardens made by the first settlers in any part of the wider world outside Europe.

Planting an orchard, indeed making any sort of garden, is an honest recognition that wherever humankind goes they change the natural environment forever. More important than what style of cultivation takes place around each home is whether or not cultivation takes place and the extent of it. Once the natural environment has been disturbed there is an obligation to look after the outcome, be it pulling out weeds along bushland walking trails, cutting fire access roads, making fire breaks, burning or removing undergrowth, right down to revegetating a barren suburban subdivision. In any case some form of tending, i.e., cultivation or gardening, takes place and this care needs to be continued. Left alone, nature will invariably reclaim the site but not necessarily with plants native to the area. It is we, not nature, who make the distinction between 'weeds' and other plants.

For most of us wanting to make a garden of some kind that provides shelter, privacy, beauty and an outdoor activity that keeps us occupied in work and thought throughout the year, a straightforward minimum-care 'landscape' is not satisfying. In a warm, dry climate an orchard garden can be the beginning of an exciting piece of gardening. It can create much-needed shade, cool microclimates, a restful setting for relaxed outdoor living and an opportunity to create a unique garden style that as yet is relatively underdeveloped.

The idea of an orchard is simple enough; a grove of productive trees, usually all the same kind or a closely related selection of cultivars, laid out in a grid pattern, trained and tended to produce a crop. On the surface of it the idea suggests a kind of plant-and-forget landscape. The trees grow, flower and fruit and the owner wanders among the trees plucking succulent, luscious ripe fruits in due season. It is, as reality proves, another of those Arcadian dreams like a garden of perpetual flowers, ever green

and lush grass lawns and rain only at night. All trees need some training and care, productive trees no less than decorative, and those that are required to provide some symmetry or formality need a good deal of attention. Those that are required to fulfil all three categories of beauty, productivity and formality need most care and attention of all. Sometimes it may seem easy to start with some specially trained and shaped trees bought in at high expense from a tree nursery, however without further regular trimming, pruning and tying in place, such things will quickly deteriorate into an ugly, unproductive and shapeless tangle. So before deciding what kind of orchard might be planted, it is wise to think how much care can be given. Or, if professional help is available, the cost in hours and cash needs to be known.

An orchard may be planned and planted, or an old one maintained and enhanced with as much eclat as any fine English flower garden. Given the natural

TOP: Nerium oleander x *'Flesh Pink'*

ABOVE: Nerium oleander x *'Tangier'*

assets and charms of tree trunks cragged with age, dappled, peeling or rugged bark, mossy roots and lichen-encrusted branches, it is not so difficult to follow the example established by the trees and make a garden simply with simple flowers and uncomplicated design that will build on the enchantment that the trees provide. Those lucky enough to have travelled in rural Provence or Italy may well know some private *bastide* or ancient *mas* where such a garden already exists. Made most often among plantations of olive, they can also be planted to almond, plum, pomegranate, peach or, where conditions allow, walnut and apple. Arabic gardens of Morocco and Spain are sometimes made within orange groves and even groves of towering date palms. Lower and less exotic trees suited to the idea could be loquats, pecans, the jujube and mulberry. Each has its own particular appeal in toothsome fruits, striking foliage, perfumed flowers and visual impact. A squadron of tall date palms may seem out of place in most landscapes but may be just the thing; a cluster of dark-leaved, black-shadowed loquats could create a heightened sense of enclosure and privacy; or a series of mulberries with tumbledown branches could recall childhood days, inviting climbing and scrambling until clothes and hands are stained indelibly with deepest red. An orchard of the same or similar kinds in tree has the strongest effect on the landscape.

Selection of plants makes a statement of ownership, possession and purpose bedded in the land and productive cultivation. It may even have something to do with the strength of the

peasant traditions of southern Europe which have led, after hundreds, if not thousands, of years to the great styles of cooking, wine-making and gardening. Epicures, gastronomists and wine-buffs searching for signs of a developing American cuisine or an Australian wine style frequently suggest that the reasons for their non-appearance is that through the post-Industrial revolution these cultures have missed out on one of the basic cultural building blocks — a strong peasant tradition. Is it not possible then

ABOVE AND LEFT: *The Judas tree,* Cercis siliquastrum, *is well-suited for planting in a grove.*

1
0
5

that by planting orchards of productive trees, suited as history shows to our particular climates, a few hesitant steps towards establishing such traditions could be made? It seems an attractive idea; one that I think is not too fanciful.

Some may say such ideas are a plastic pastiche that skips the evolutionary stage in favour of establishing some fashionable (and transient) vogue. This could happen, of course, but when we look around we see among the outer suburbs of our towns and cities the derelict remnants of orchards and truck gardens that already give the necessary clues about what to grow. There is a history of husbandry and land use already near at hand, but instead of acknowledging these emergent traditions, accepting and refining them we tend to sweep them away utterly and replace them with some contrived landscape, derivative of some distant idealised Romantic and unsuited fashion. Looking about my own city, I can see areas where olives were once cultivated along the dry, stony foothills; elsewhere orange groves lined the banks of the one semi-permanent stream; stone fruits flourished on the floodplains and vineyards were everywhere abundant.

Getting back to orchards as the backbone of a garden plan, it must be admitted that they are more formal in appearance than present gardening fashions accustom us to feel is proper. So some transitional ideas may be useful to bridge the gap between those attracted to the idea as one suited to their climatic circumstances and those who can admit the sensibility of the idea but yet have their reservations about leading the way outside the scope of fashionable gardening. It is interesting here to consider the fashion pages of any up-market glossy magazine. Do the couturiers not speak about 'exploring the possibilities', 'expanding the boundaries' and 'enlarging the vision' of their craft? How dull in comparison to read garden designers' assurances to their readers that their offerings follow the latest style. Duller still, that one style is pushed relentlessly as the one style more beautiful, more admirable, superior and international in its application than any other. Lacking conviction and confidence to develop their own creations in response to their needs and their environment, how many are forever bound to the endless cycle of fashion? Fashion victims in gardening have in the last thirty years been swept through Japanese gardens, native gardens, California gardens, English flower gardens, cottage gardens, Jekyll gardens, formal French gardens, Sissinghurst gardens, Tex-Mex gardens, Hidcote gardens, 'new' English flower gardens, wild gardens, post-Modern gardens and Mediterranean gardens — all in the name of discovering the one unique true self-perpetuating, low maintenance take-your-breath-away every time style. And it has always turned out to be bunkum.

Following every landscape design conference, following each glossy 'super' book and every magnificent television series comes a new turn of the wheel of gardening fashions. It has almost become an annual change. Looking ahead a few years, could it be that new garden fashions will be launched with all the pizzazz and exclusive secrecy of a Parisian haute couture spring collection? Will the new garden designs be constructed in some locked pavilion with admission only by gilt-edged card on the day? Will anxious designers dressed in casual suave or radical chic vie for television and media coverage? Will the papparazzi fight to get admitted? Will an elite of glitterati attend the openings of their favourite designers? Could it be that this happens already at . . . hush!

There is, of course nothing to prevent orchard gardens becoming last year's vogue. Nothing unless it makes sense to your climate and lifestyle. Then the shade and cool of a garden that gives respite from the brightest sunshine and the most infernal heat recommends an orchard as a great starting point for a garden; one that becomes part of our living space and an asset to an outdoor lifestyle. When a garden becomes so comfortable that it is part of daily life it has a fair chance of avoiding the deadly tag of being the latest fashion. It does not need changing because it doesn't suit. It is above fashion. It may even be an expression of life as art.

My own garden is made in the remains of an old apple orchard, but on the warmer, drier plains below our hills olive trees have flourished for nearly two hundred years. So well do they grow that they have naturalised widely; self-sown and spread by birds they form dense thickets of brush that yearly attract the attention of wild food gatherers from the city and suburbs. The small fruits are harvested for pickling and for pressing. More recently, larger fruited cultivars such as Manzanilla, Gordal and Mission have been planted or grafted onto older trees. These are good to eat and make wonderful oil, but it is the oldest trees which appeal to me. Their gnarled trunks and knotted root buttresses clothed in smooth grey-green bark are living sculptures that instantly draw the eye and beckon the hand to stroke.

I should have no difficulty making a garden in a grove of such venerable trees. It would be simple so as not to detract from the beauty of the trees, and it would be drought-tolerant so as not to endanger the trees by overwatering. Perhaps its boundary would be marked by a rubble wall, rounded at the top and roughly smoothed over with pale sandy concrete such as were once made hereabouts. Perhaps a hedge of bay or plumbago would serve instead. Within, shaded by the trees and screened from view, a table and some rough garden seats formed from stones and concrete and softened with cushions would form the focal point. Around the sitting-out space, rosemaries in variety

would find a home, along with hairy-leaved oregano, winter savoury, the toughest of thymes and garlic chives. Maintaining a sense of very casual gardening, the approach to the seats would be lined with artemisias and scented-leaf geraniums, shrubby and prostrate forms of each.

Sensitivity is required to create seasonal colour in such a simple garden. Bearing in mind that summer watering would defeat the purpose of creating an orchard garden, and could well endanger the trees if it were applied in the volume needed to keep flowers going all through summer, a dashing display of the simplest hardy bulbs under the trees would suffice for spring and for the rest of the year large pots of flowers around the sitting-out area would be all that was needed. In the backgound the silvered foliage of the olives and their fantastic trunks, and the silvery pale gold grasses underneath

A striking *display of* *potted* Hippeastrum *hybrids such as* *these adds a* *bold colour* *note against a* *background of* *trees and grass.*

would be a quiet foil to the livelier foreground.

For bulbs that would thrive in the short grass under the trees I would look to the brilliant winter-flowering bulbs of South Africa: sparaxis, babiana, freesia, geissorhiza, tritonia, morea, oxalis and romulea. Fleshy bulbs which habitually grow above the soil such as veltheimia, eucomis and nerine would not tolerate mowing so should be avoided in this situation. But the others could be planted in drifts as large as can be raised or afforded. By mid-summer the foliage will have begun to yellow and the ripe seeds been broadcast by their bursting pods so a run-over with the lawn mower set 5 cm or so high will tidy up the orchard ready for the drier months.

Potted colour can be as splendid or as simple as you wish. For me pots represent summer heartache unless they are managed carefully and well tended. My first preference is for pots as large as can be afforded — something the size of an Italian lemon-tree pot offers lots of scope for imaginative planting and is easy to keep watered. It also allows the possiblity of using plants grown on in plastic pots to drop into the decorative terracotta pieces as flowers and foliage fade and the decor needs to be rejuvenated with replacement plants. My second preference is for fewer flowers and more foliage. Two groups of pots that stand at our front door and by our back door contain nothing but hostas. This is an old idea: Gertrude Jekyll showed photographs of her own such plantings in her book *Home and Garden* of 1900 and I have seen them in many other gardens grown this way. The hosta foliage lasts all summer long and serves to show off pots of lilies and other exotica that flower for a much shorter time. Tubs of *Lilium* x 'Golden Clarion', 'Black Beauty' and pink and white Oriental seedlings pass in parade along with *Gloriosa rothschildiana* and *Sandersonia aurantica* while the hostas stand by. These have recently been joined by a small selection of vireya rhododendrons that have good evergreen leaves as well as pretty flowers. To match the lilies I chose pale shades such as cream ('Buttermilk' and 'Gardenia') and pale pink ('Penrice' and 'Pink Delight'), but for the solo hostas by the back door I picked out brighter-coloured forms like 'Nuginea Red', 'Orange Wax' and 'Celebration'.

These may not do for planting at the heart of an orchard, though I have seen large pots of hostas used in such a setting, but a series of very large pots can hold an impressive, simple and changing display. Something as simple as the bronze-leaved *Carex petriei* could be the constant feature in a changing pot of other reddish and bronze-toned plants. It would be fun to try out the possible combinations of dahlias 'Bishop of Llandaff' and 'Yellow Hammer', *Cosmos atrosanguineus*, bronze-coloured Asiatic *Lilium* hybrids, dwarf dark-leaved New Zealand

A grove of old olive trees enhanced with simple bulbs

1
0
9

flaxes such as 'Elfin', 'Thumbelina' and 'Bronze Baby' and even the black-leaved *Ophiopogon planiscapus* 'Nirgrescens'. Sub-shrubs like *Salvia greggii* 'Raspberry Royal' would look well in partnership with colours such as these. Smart topiarists could add small lollipops carved from *Berberis thunbergii* 'Helmond Pillar' while more casual folk might be statisfied with *Coprosma* 'Walter Brockie' and the downright light-hearted could go for a less studied composition with something like *Ballota pseudodictamnus*, *Astelia nervosa* 'Alpine Ruby' or *Helichrysum petiolare.*

If you are the kind of gardener who can control the urge to grow ever more kinds of plants with a more disciplined enjoyment of simple things, a collection of red or pink geraniums, or white if your sensibilities are more delicate, would give telling colour and Mediterranean simplicity with minimal care. Succulent plants like *Aeonium arboreum* 'Zwartkop', *Agave parrassana* and forms of *Cotyledon orbiculata*, *Dudleya* spp. and large *Echeveria* hybrids could also add to the overall impact of bold forms and coloured leaves, as could semi-tropical plants such as datura and ricinus; plants which need double care to ensure that their poisonous parts don't endanger anyone.

Herb-minded gardeners could add strong colours using the many purple-leaved forms of basil that are now getting about. These with the bronze fennel offer more variety of leaf shape and plant form to play about with; though it would be folly to think that there would be enough to cut for regular use in the kitchen in such decorative schemes. After all, you can't eat the stuff and look at it admiringly in the garden too!

The most important consideration is not to have too many pots; four of the largest size should be enough for the most ambitious gardener. The cost of large pots may seem daunting, but to me they seem worth the price. I have only two, and have plans to buy two more. There need be no more. Enough is enough; another case of less is more. If plants seem like more work than can be comfortably contemplated in the heat of high summer there are still other, easier options which still look great so long as you carry off the ideas with *bravura.* Piling the pots high with pyramids of pine cones, shells or rocks creates a very theatrical effect so long as the objects used are carefully selected for their visual qualities. To my untrained artistic eye, it seems preferable to keep the basic construction materials all of a kind, of similar size, colour and texture with just a scattering of smaller pieces to add piquancy, and to bolster the cohesion of the structure. It is possible not to have anything housed in such large pots; they have ample *gravitas* of their own — especially the more luxuriantly decorated sorts such as come from Italy. We are fortunate in having a local maker of 'Tuscan' pots who

1
1
0

decorates his wares with low relief bands of gum leaves; a nice local touch which perhaps may be done with motifs familiar to other places. The scale of such pots calls for standard citrus trees, oleanders or cycads, but such things are not always available in sizes to match the containers, and they do need attentive watering lest dryness at the roots and high rates of transpiration cause the plants to droop and become distressed. Plants with few leaves won't do, so maybe are best done without if a daily round and watering where needed are not possible, or likely.

The presence of big pots relies on more than size; the decorative masks, swags and deeply moulded rims create rich patterns that are strengthened as they get older by stains, lichens, mosses and the patina of old terracotta. For me the delight of such a thing is in its own character and the romance of its manufacture; simple forms may well be made by machinery but the more elaborate kinds are still made by hand on a massive foot-operated potter's wheel and the moulded decorative pieces applied later. Yet others are built up from thick coils of clay pressed and smoothed over a collapsible wooden frame that supports a rope laid against it loop on loop to form a rough mould. The potter works the clay on the outfacing surface of rope until the form is complete. When the clay has dried out for some time the wooden form is knocked down and lifted out; the rope pulled out and the free form of the pot is ready for the kiln. To watch such operations is indeed to see an ancient cultural tradition that still lives in the hands of a few artisans. To have such a thing in my garden is a pleasure in itself. In a very different vein are pots covered with a bright mosaic of broken tiles, or more recent versions which may be gay with broken mirror, shards of china plates, pretty shells and interesting rocks. A bold imagination could plant such pots with a multi-hued riot of brightly coloured annuals, or with mixed flowers all of a single primary colour. Then again a mixture of succulents could produce surprising effects, and hardy geraniums always look good. But should we not get back to thinking about orchards? I think so.

Besides proper orchards of productive trees, the idea of an orchard can be carried by regular plantations of flowering trees such a the Judas tree (*Cercis siliquastrum*), western redbud (*Cercis occidentalis*) and oleander (*Nerium oleander*) planted in groves. To be effective grown in this manner, small shrublike trees such as these must be thoughtfully trained by pruning and short-term staking to ensure that they develop a single tall standard stem. This is not the natural habit of such trees, but encouraged by your caring attentions they will quickly respond and grow into trees that can be sat under. The oleander is very prone to sprouting new growths from the base of the main trunk and these need to be removed

ABOVE: *The low sprawling form of Mexican sage,* Salvia leucantha, *makes an attractive companion plant to other silver and grey-leaved plants.*

RIGHT: Nerium oleander *x 'Soeur Agnes'*

ruthlessly and regularly. A small amount of work for the pleasure of sitting out under a canopy of flowers. I am particularly attracted to the idea of creating a bower with alternate pink and white plants of oleander, though a similar planting of white and cream forms, or pink and apricot, or white and apricot would all offer colour schemes with endless combinations of flowering plants underneath. Crepe myrtles (cultivars of *Lagerstroemia indica*) could also be used in this manner to great effect, and they possess the bonus of lovely smooth, mottled bark. In some areas the leaves will also develop bright red and orange autumn tones.

Sometimes a whole orchard can feel claustrophobic. This is especially so if the whole garden has no outlook, either by being totally screened from the outside by its own foliage or if the canopy is particularly dense, as may be the case if loquats (*Eriobotrya japonica*) were chosen to carry out the plan. Fear of overdoing things can be assuaged by adopting a variation on the orchard theme: the quincunx. This peculiar-sounding thing is in fact a simple double row of trees planted in a square pattern to leave an empty space in the middle of the plantation. Commonsense decrees that such a space could be small enough for a piece of sculpture and a patch of cobbling, or large enough to set up a market umbrella, table and chairs. Do not leave the alley between the paired rows of trees unused. This can be turned into a delightful cool tunnel for strolling if it is large, or for children to play hide-and-seek if it is smaller. Again, some careful pruning and training will be needed, but never let that thought put off the long-term pleasure of such a garden.

It is but a short step from this idea to another even simpler and yet little used in small gardens where it could be used effectively to screen out unwanted, intrusive sights and focus attention firmly on something attractive. I refer to the potential of avenues. I do not mean long plantations of massive oaks, or even the equally impressive lines of palms sometimes found in large gardens where climates are warm. I mean something much closer to the earth and more suited to the needs of small gardens. Any of the compact shrubby trees discussed already could be well deployed to make an avenue in a small garden. Trained very formally, and maybe clipped to maintain a tight canopy, the product would be akin to a pleached allee so beloved by devotees of the modern English flower garden but also much used, if not the subject of such high praise, by Mediterranean gardeners. Treated less strictly, the effect is much closer to a simple grove. Plainly, the more manicured the plantation the more elaborate can be the hardware and plantings that accompany it. But even in this case, perhaps it is wise to eschew the floriferous attractions of a full-blown perennial border or some other equally lush garden. We would not wish to fall back to old habits by imagining that we could overcome the realities of our warm, dry climates and by hard work and great expense transport our own little patch of garden to some other greener place; look instead to the garden traditions of climates similar to our own, understanding that we are looking not to copy them but to find the spark to ignite our own ideas.

1
1
3

A GARDEN WITH

quiet waters

There is almost no Chamber but it hath at its Door

a Storehouse of running water; that 'tis full of

Parterres, pleasant Walks, shady Places, Rivolets,

Fountains, Jets of Water, Grottas, great Caves against

the heat of the day, and great Terrasses raised high, and very airy, to sleep upon

in the cool: in a word, you know not there what 'tis to be hot.

Francois Bernier

Collection of *Travels through Turkey into Persia and the East Indies...... being the travels of Monsieur Tavernier Bernier and other great men.* Published for Moses Pitt at The Angel in St Paul's Churchyard, London, 1684.

'Knowing not what 'tis to be hot'; what an admirable ambition for any gardener striving to make a garden that is a haven in the heat and drought of summer. Having managed to set aside old ideas about the progress of the seasons, and indeed the names and number of seasons, and having decided to follow the patterns of growth and

PREVIOUS PAGES:

(p. 114)

*A Moorish-
style fountain,
basin and
runnel set
against a
background of
clipped greens
make an apt
setting for
potted
rosemary,
lavender and
citrus trees at
Lotusland in
Santa Barbara,
California.*

(p. 115)

Heliotropium *x
'Lord Roberts'*

floraison that accord with the local environment, there is still the psychological effect of the hot weather to counteract in any place where the summers are hot and dry and dusty. Monsieur Bernier was delighted to discover the ingenuity with which the Mughal emperors of India overcame the stifling heat and lassitude brought on by the arrival of summer in northern India. The water gardens made by Babur, Humayun, Akbar, Jahangir, Shah Jahan and Aurangzib in the 16th and 17th centuries as they moved with their armies and courts through Hindustan and Kashmir have remained as amazing examples of a style of garden making in response to an inhospitable climate. Within a framework based on the teachings of Mohammed and Islamic culture, these gardens were designed as earthly representations of the pleasures of Paradise and as such are dwelling places in themselves just as Paradise is the dwelling place of the soul.

How unlike the other great water gardens made at approximately the same time: the water gardens of the Italian Renaissance at Villa d'Este, Villa Lante, Villa Aldobrandini where the focal point of the garden is the house and the garden itself a tool and demonstration of the earthly power of those Cardinal princes of the Church who commanded their construction. Where the Mughals maintained the natural forms of water itself — still reflecting surfaces, burbling springs, chattering cascades — and used it in fairly restrained quantities, the Italian prelates controlled water through elaborate hydraulic works and compelled it through symbolic sculptures to gush, spout, roar and foam. The Mughal emperors and the Cardinals both used their gardens as a background to the ceremonial of their courts; and again the atmosphere established in each case is quite different.

No doubt both kinds of gardens were the venue of all kinds of courtly intrigue and nasty business, but in one case petitioners to the court were invited to share, however briefly, a vision of earthly Paradise; the other garden was probably more like a waiting room with the trappings and signs of vast personal power on show to suitably impress mendicants. While the subtleties of power and patronage expressed by the approach to the use of water in gardens in both cultures now seems very distant and unrelated to present-day gardening, we should not forget the impact of these gardens on us. Without any understanding of the times in which they were made, the response they produce in us can still be profound and provide insights into ways in which our gardens might be made enjoyable living spaces despite a climate that appears inhospitable and without promise to those whose acculturation is based largely in northern Europe.

Not having the wealth or power these days either to take control of large pieces of land and divert entire watersheds, or to commandeer armies of engineers, sculptors, labourers and gardeners, it could be wondered just what these Mughal water gardens might inspire in us, or what those of Italy may animate in our minds for that matter.

Both psychologically and physically, water gardens engender refreshment of the mind and body; especially so in climates that are harsh and hot for months on end. The sight and sound of water, even the suggestion of it can lift a sagging spirit at the end of a day spent in heatwave conditions. Instinctively, at the sight of water in a garden we reach to touch and feel its cool and soothing qualities. On hot days do we not instinctively trail our hands in troughs and the basins of fountains, or splash our hands under the squirt of a sprinkler? Given the chance, do we need permission to slip off our shoes and socks and dunk our hot feet in a puddle, or dangle them from some convenient perch into a pool? The sensuous qualities of water are undeniable. It is the very essence of 'cool'. More than that, the sounds serve to remind us of the coolness of water, even though we may not have time to perform any of the above acts, or to find a water hole large enough to dive in and swim about. In the heat of summer it is not necessary to hear the roar of a might waterfall or to be drenched to shivering by the spray of a raging torrent to know the restorative powers of water. The merest drip, quietly plopping into a shallow basin is sufficient to stir our memory banks and release an anticipatory tingle of cool sensation.

The particularly impressive achievement of the Mughal designers was that with quite small quantities of water and small flow rates they imagined and contrived a variety of means of reproducing all the pleasant, stimulatory sensations water can generate. Without the benefit of complex technology they were able to take a small stream and introduce it to a stylised garden sequence. Included within its formally arrayed components may have been still reflective pools, some large enough to contain small square islands and pavilions, connecting bridges that 'floated' just above the water level; low burbling fountains, foaming chattering cascades (*chadars*), tinkling rills, still-running canals, and limpid bathing tanks. Stonework was often contrived so as to allow places to sit directly over the brink of some small drop so that a contemplative soul could find refreshment from the cool air created by the proximity of the tumbling waters. Animation was introduced by the play of water and the sparkle of sunlight flashing from simple 'peacock's tail' water jets and from coloured carp which were often introduced to the pools. It seems unlikely that many of us would be able to indulge ourselves by having any fish we might possess kitted out with gold lip rings, with or without pearls or bells attached, but like the Mughals we can derive considerable invigoration by sitting, eating and even sleeping near water. According to the manner in which it is deployed in a garden, water alone seems able to bring about feelings of seclusion and serenity. These are sensations which heighten the coolness created by evaporating water. It seems to me that people in any hot, arid place are most susceptible to these restorative qualities in late afternoon and early evening, when after a day at work a time should be made for quiet relaxation in a serene and secluded setting.

Of course it doesn't always work out that way; if the water is in the form of a swimming pool, sometimes the scene will be filled with boisterous activity. But what matter? There will be many times when there are no crowds of shrieking teenagers and no bawling children. When the pool is still and the garden quiet, this is the time to slide gently into the water and leave behind the concerns of the day.

Most of us will find that the water garden to which we aspire will take the form of a swimming pool. This does not, however confine thinking, planning or construction to a rectangle of bare cement with a rim of vivid blue tiles and a volume of even more startling sky-blue water. No matter what any swimming pool salesperson says, do not be persuaded that this ugly and common model of pool is the only practical way to have a swimming pool. Imagine how modern swimming pools could be so much more; more than an expensive hole in the ground; more than a splash of unnaturally blue water, and more than a place to swim lap after

A standard of
Alogyne
huegelii x
'Santa Cruz'

breathless lap. After the initial enthusiasm of pool ownership wears off it is too easy for them to become a dominant but ineffectual, and little-used feature in a garden. Children may swear mighty promises, but rarely live up to their oaths to help keep the thing clean and quite soon decide that adolescent friendships are much to be preferred over family togetherness, and moreover are best conducted somewhere else. Eventually the hapless owner, most often one who doesn't do all that much swimming anyway, is left with an increasingly hateful object; generator of unwanted work and consumer of much valuable time. Schemes to be rid of the thing begin to hatch and that is why a little more thought at the beginning will pay off.

Do we really need an Olympic-length pool? Does it have to be finished in white? Do we want to swim or just get wet and cool on a hot day? How can a swimming pool be more effectively integrated into a garden? But enough of this. I have been through it all and can say there are some simple means of making a swimming pool less of an eyesore and more a part of a garden. The first consideration should be to reduce in so far as possible the most blatant feature: the brilliant blueness of the water. It is positively unnatural and impinges severely upon any impact a garden may have, especially its serenity. Now that a choice of colours can be made concerning the finish of the inside of the pool, it is possible, and desirable, to choose some dark colour that will provide a more restful background. If possible some thought can be given to screening the pool from other parts of the garden; this can provide a very useful suntrap, creates a greater degree of privacy and can make the pool area secure should a child-proof area around the swimming pool be required.

A traditional Spanish-American fountain sets a tone of simplicity and calm in the patio at Mission San Carlos Borromeo de Carmelo, California.

With most filtration systems it is possible to include additional water-return pipes to the pool from the filter. By this means small spouts or fountains can be included in the design; the scope for imaginative development of this idea ranges through all the examples provided by the old gardens of Spain, Italy and India. My best advice could be to keep

1
1
9

such devices simple; a single spout from a stone dolphin or lion mask, a row of small jets arching into the main body of water from the edge of the pool, or a small flow over a carved shell basin will be enough to suggest other gardens in other places and go some way towards taking attention away from the utilitarian purposes of the pool. Slightly more elaborate constructions could include ideas that enable sitting over the water or surrounded by it as in the examples provided by the great Mughal emperors. Considering the elaborate 'Hawaiian' style lagoon pools which include in-water drinks bars and swim-in eating areas it would seem probable that equally imaginative ideas could be built into swimming pool designs without challenging convention too much. For instance, a small pool and bubbling spout connected to the main pool by a shallow rill could follow the Mughal tradition by being placed within a summer house or poolside shelter. If the paving dropped down a step or two towards the swimming pool an opportunity would arise for some simple cascades to be constructed within the rill; a sheet of copper placed across the water course at right angles where the paving levels change would create a solid sheet of water cascading over the lip of the metal and down to the next level. The sight and sound would be delightful and refreshing. Marble, jasper and porphyry, as used to make water gardens by the Moors and Mughals, may be out of reach but the ideas are not.

I have seen one good example of an old swimming pool converted to other uses by an owner whose family had grown up and left home. I am sure there must be many similar examples of creative thinking on the subject. At Erambie, a pastoral property near Orange in New South Wales, a large, rectangular swimming pool has been made into a very successful lily pool by its owner, Mrs Mary Glasson. Fortunately the pool was designed on very simple lines and by removing the stainless steel pool ladder and mounts for the diving board things were ready for a speedy conversion. With the help of a farm-hand cum gardener the pool was two-thirds filled with crushed rock; coarse gravel about fist-sized, and large plastic rubbish bins filled with soil and planted up with a selection of waterlilies were sunk below the water line. It was found necessary to anchor the bins firmly by wedging them among the rocks, but otherwise a simple, if wet, task. The addition of a trio of bronze cranes at one end of the pool and a small summer house at the other end has completed a very satisfactory garden composition. The effect is relaxing and the work required to maintain it is easily manageable; all that needs to be done is an occasional topping up of the water, the removal of dead lily pads and an application of fertiliser when the plants' energy for growth slows. Several of the strongest-growing varieties have required lifting, dividing and repotting in the ten or so years the pool has been used in this way. All in all a most engaging piece of water gardening.

This may seem like pretty rich stuff, so let us consider some much simpler means by which water can be included in a garden.

An idea which I have followed for years is to keep a number of goldfish in a very large Thai storage pot. It is glazed inside and out with a pleasant shade of soft green and has no drainage hole in the bottom, but a small outlet on the side very near the bottom. Its was probably intended for use as a storage for fresh water for a household, or perhaps as a container for fermenting fish sauce or some other such product of Asian cuisine, but it serves admirably as a fish tank. The hole has been plugged with a small cork and the pot filled with water. It variously holds three to seven fish, depending on the attentions of local predatory birds and the hardiness of the fish. From time to time the fish are netted out and the whole thing emptied and scrubbed clean of slime. It is a simple idea that brings a small corner of the garden to life with the sparkle of the sun on the water and the lazy movement of the fish. There have been times when I have contemplated other ways of using such a large pot to grow plants of the sacred lotus (*Nelumbo nucifera*) or dwarf waterlilies. So far I have resisted having more than one such pot, but the idea bears consideration. It would work even in a very small courtyard.

Suitable varieties for planting in containers like these could be *Nelumbo nucifera* 'Momo Botan', a dwarf, double-pink form of the sacred lotus, or *Nelumbo nucifera* 'Shiroman', a large creamy white-flowered form; there are others too, such as 'Mrs Perry Slocum' which has flowers that show a range of colours from cream through pink to apricot, and there is the usual form *Nelumbo nucifera* 'Roseum Plenum'. Choice dwarf waterlilies are found in *Nymphaea x* 'Indiana' (deep orange-red), *Nymphaea x* 'Tetragona Alba' (white), *Nymphaea x* 'Aurora' (soft apricot), *Nymphaea x* 'Pink Laydeker' (rich rose-pink) and *Nymphaea x* 'Helvola' (very small yellow). Should the idea of water gardening on this intimate scale take hold, then other plants such as *Acorus gramineus* 'Variegatus', *Pontederia cordata, Ranunculus lingua* 'Grandiflorus' and any number of papyri, sedges and rushes will support a fertile imagination in planning watery gardens of delight.

Rills are something virtually unknown to many gardeners, having fallen from the fashionable heights they once enjoyed through garden designers such as Gertrude Jekyll and Sir Edwin Lutyens. The concept has been known at least since Moorish times in Spain, but may well go back to ancient Egyptian gardens. The Patio de la Acequia (the Court of the Canal) in the Generalife palace in Granada is probably the best-known example of an early rill garden and well known to tourists, though within the Generalife-Alhambra complex of gardens are many smaller rills which supply water to various parts of the gardens. Basically, a rill is a very small streamlet. In most instances

The beauty of the Patio de La Aciequa at the Generalife garden palace in Granada, Spain has inspired many garden designers with its relaxed atmosphere.

in gardens it is taken to be a small flow of water contained within a straight course (though sometimes meandering or serpentine) by stone walls. It can be seen as a direct descendent of the earliest mud-walled canals which delivered a trickle of water to rows of plants at the end of an irrigation system. The Moorish sultans, the Mughal emperors, Hindustani rajahs and many other early makers of leisure gardens designed their creations around a formalised, stylised version of an irrigation system, gardens becoming more complex as the centuries passed. In England at the close of the 19th century Miss Jekyll and her collaborator Sir Edwin Lutyens designed several gardens wherein the rill played a central role in unifying the design. Gardens such as those at The Deanery and Hestercombe show how effective use can be made of a very small flow of water, contained within a stone-or brick-lined channels, that may connect a series of small pools and be fed at one end by a small fountain. Though highly decorative and richly planted with all manner of water plants and marginal plants, the water served some practical purpose too, at least in theory, for the pools were often designated as 'dipping pools' which were used to draw water for watering numerous potted plants displayed at strategic points about the gardens. As a garden device, it makes a big impact for a comparatively small outlay. It is odd that it has not been made greater use of by designers in recent years. Without doubt there is work involved in maintenance, but the sight of even a small quantity of water in a garden is so attractive that a rill should be thought of as one way in which water can be introduced into gardens without having the necessity of a large volume of water, or a place to put it!

Another simple idea seems to have been drawn in part from the Islamic requirement for ritual hand-washing before prayers and takes the form of a shallow pool with a gentle overflow into a catchment below. A circular pool arranged with a lip and lower basin is often found in the forecourts of mosques and allows worshippers to wash their hands as required. Translated into a purely decorative function in a garden this arrangement can be replicated by a simple stone cube carved with a shallow trough and with a bubbler inset at its centre. The water flows through the bubbler filling the trough

and overflows from the edges of the cube into a shallow catchment beneath. An idea as simple as this could easily be made up using a block of the soft black lava stone such as comes presently from Java. Those exported display ornate carving, but a much simpler, plainer style of design could easily be commissioned through the wholesale traders who import such wares. That the stone is extremely porous is of no

concern, indeed it could well be an asset if the constantly damp stone becomes host to any fern or moss sporlings. The overflow water can be collected by a cement-lined sump filled with small gravel at the base of the stone block and the water reticulated by a small pump.

1
2
3

PREVIOUS PAGE:

The gentle

play of water

from this

Colebrookdale

fountain

enlivens a

peaceful

garden in

Hobart,

Australia (top).

The

languorous

form of

Crinum *x*

Powellii *'Alba'*

(bottom)

Building on that idea, what about replacing the stone block with a piece of sculpture or pottery? There are no doubt many fine artists in our communities who would be glad of the chance to create a small piece to your commission. With art galleries and craft galleries, exhibitions and fairs proliferating on every hand it should be possible to find a person whose work you admire and to lay your desires before them. Provided that you have a clear idea of the costs involved and a reasonable understanding about how long the creative process will take, it is not beyond the ability of most people to spell out their requirements in a commission. In essence you need a figurative or non-figurative work, according to your preference, in a durable material that will be long lasting outdoors with water playing over it. Whatever design is proposed by the artist must be capable of having built into it a means of delivering a small spout or trickle of water — again it is your decision to determine which, and it must be stable with some means of ensuring that it can be discreetly attached to some other hidden cement or stone footing. It is surprising how determined and daring some petty criminals can be about 'lifting' small items of garden art, so it pays to make sure that whatever piece you have will not easily be carried off. If a commission seems beyond reach, though they are often not as expensive as might be imagined, there are alternatives in converting a large, decorative terracotta urn or jar into a water feature. Any deft handyperson should be able to bore through the base of such an object and insert a short length of copper tubing to deliver water as a small jet or bubbler at the mouth of the pot. To keep the whole thing stable the tube can be held in place by partially filling the pot with cement. The only disadvantage to this method is that running repairs at a later date will probably be impossible without smashing the pot. Packing the pot after the tube is in place with small gravel would most likely serve just as well. The overflow can drop onto a bed of loose pebbles and hence into a sump where it can be gathered and recirculated by a small pump.

A reverse idea could also be considered where a small jet of water could be directed at a piece of sculpture or pottery and then fall into a pebble-covered sump. To achieve the best effect, and to save the water splashing all over the garden, a relatively flat surface carved in bas-relief or with a shallow patterns may be the best to look for when selecting a piece to build into the garden. Those who have been lucky enough to visit the gardens made by Rosemary Verey at Barnsley House, in Gloucestershire, may recall a delightful fountain based on a bas-relief sculpture of sheep by Simon Verity; several small spouts of water play onto the face of the sculpted slab and trickle water into a small basin below half hidden by lush growth. That is the sort of idea I have in

1

2

4

mind. In the case of a garden in a hot climate, the lush growth might usefully be reduced to one or two plants with bold foliage such as *Acanthus spinosus* or *Iris pseudacorus* 'Variegata', or maybe a favourite cultivar of *Hemerocallis* paired with the giant fennel (*Ferula communis*). Something as bold as *Miscanthus sinensis* 'Gracillimus' juxtaposed with the red-leaved, pink-veined *Canna* x 'Durban' (syn. *Canna* x 'Tropicana' in Australia) or maybe foiled by the purple foliage of *Crinum* x 'Powellii Purpurea' would not be amiss. Nothing more would be needed to make a very telling piece of gardening. Enough is enough. The whole could be set in a bed of gravel that would conceal a water-saving sump at the base of the sculpture, making a minimalist statement to perfection.

Problems, problems, problems, that is all some garden-makers ever see. What a load of problems a water garden of any sort can bring; mosquitoes, frogs, pesky invasive water weeds, muck and mud, bad smells, slop, sludge and slime, fallen leaves, fallen leaves and more fallen leaves to be scooped out before they clog up the works. Why go to all the bother? Looked on from such a negative aspect almost every piece of garden is just one load of nuisance chores after another. Why bother to garden at all? A decent slab of green cement would answer just as well and wouldn't be half the work to keep clean! Indeed, why bother? We bother because we love to garden and need to have that contact with the soil and with the rhythms and seasons of the natural world, and because the work is enjoyable and because the results of bothering to garden are pleasing to us and to those about whom we care.

There is no doubt that any sort of water garden creates work, just like any other kind of gardening. Yes, the leaves will have to be cleaned out whether it be from a swimming pool or from a tiny fish pond, but I doubt the quantity of work is any greater than that required to keep grass neat or to sweep clean a cement slab. Totted up over the year, the total time taken has to be evaluated against the amount of pleasure derived; if the sensations and activities attached to a water garden are significant then, as with any other piece of gardening, the work entailed is easily warranted by the outcome.

"All these palaces are full of gardens with running water, which flows in channels into reservoirs of stone, jasper and marble. In all the rooms and halls of these palaces there are ordinary fountains or reservoirs of the same stone of proportionate size. In the gardens of these palaces there are always flowers according to the season. In these palaces are seats and private rooms, some of which are in the midst of the running water. In the water are many fish for delight."

Niccolao Manucci

Storia do Mogor

translated by W Irvine. (London: John Murray, 1907, from the first edition of 1705.)

1
2
5

L E S S O N S   I N
stones

One of the most significant differences between the idyllic gardens which are so familiar to us through a multitude of illustrated books and the reality of gardening in places where the sun shines hot, strong and long is the magnificence of the lawns. Rich and lush they unroll like ribbons and sheets of green through the glorious gardens of Normandy, Gloucestershire and Connecticut.

Such perfection; velvety, uniformly green and not a weed anywhere to disturb the unifying impact of the emerald carpet as it moves through woodland, fronts perennial borders and spreads in full glory in front of a suitably impressive house. It is such a pervasive image, and one so powerful in our perception of what a garden should be. It is an image encouraged by environmental journalists, by massive promotional campaigns in the interest of chemical companies, real estate developers, sports

PREVIOUS PAGES:

(p. 126)

A striking red-

painted wall

sets off a

troupe of

potted

conifers,

Tanghua

Temple,

Kunming,

China.

(p. 127) Gazania

x 'Mitsuwa'.

promoters and other conspiratorial types; not to mention numerous goody-goodies and nosy bods who insist on some sort of communal tidiness that indicates high-minded morality and decency. In America, where such pure and green images are enforced by community bylaws and resisted by subversive urban renegades like Michael Pollan (*Second Nature — a gardener's education*. New York: Laurel/Dell/Doubleday, 1991) the pervasive pressure to have green carpets from 'shore to golden shore' has given rise to a proliferation of green that has even smothered parts of the Mojave and Sonoran Deserts. That entire river systems have been diverted from such unproductive activities as market-gardening and fruit growing is of little consequence considered alongside the economic advantages of pursuing little white balls around a field with sticks! Lawns, swards, sweeps, greens, verges, strips, plats — how the stuff has proliferated, diversified and multiplied since the days when it was just plain grass.

In countries where water-wise gardening is necessary, lawns and grass can create a most worrisome headache for many gardeners. They just won't stay green all year. Even with massive and frequent irrigation throughout the months of heat and drought the darn stuff simply looks ratty. Despite application of all manner of fertilisers, lawn foods and chemicals the turf looks tatty. To preserve sanity, home owners eventually begin to lose interest in a battle they can never win and begin to find interests other than lawns on which to expend their energies and enthusiasms. Some utterly reject gardening and turn to the pleasures of the flesh, others give thought to how they can garden without lawns, and how they can reduce the amount of grass that they have in their gardens. Notice that I differentiate between lawn and grass. The distinctions are clear when you think about it — lawn is lavished with care, manicured, fed and watered regularly; grass is not, it is just grass. It may be mown occasionally to keep it under control, and it may even be weeded of its larger-leaved constituents so that it looks reasonably uniform when it goes yellow and dries off. At least that is my preference, but it doesn't have to be yours. Deciding to have grass instead of lawn is usually just the first phase of a progression towards a garden in which the area of grass is lessened and replaced with other surfaces. It is an important and crucial step. Feeling comfortable about having yellowed grass, with or without dandelions, during the dry months of the year is also about beginning to feel culturally at home in a land that is not green during summer.

It has been usual for this step to take place after the children of a family have grown up and no longer need the large areas of lawn to play on that we have been conditioned to think they cannot develop normal play and socialisation without. That children in other cultures managed to grow up without lawn obviously meant they didn't play games, are socially maladjusted and are probably in need of many heavy sessions of lawn therapy. In the last few years that thinking has changed. Children will play no matter what. And we can do without lawns and still garden handsomely.

Should melancholia set in while this realisation is working its way towards acceptance by your innermost heart, there are remedies (see The Time to Plant Crocuses, page 191). Happily there are now more and more gardens which give ample evidence that lawns can be done without and that quite small areas of grass are sufficient for normal family development.

Of all things in a garden, lawn and grass are perhaps the most demanding of time, energy and resources to keep at a level of appearance that is presentable and useful. That is, it looks green, is tidy and weed free. Even if a decision is made not to worry too much if the grass is dormant and yellow in summer, it still needs to look well cared for, and indeed if it is expected that it will return to verdure when the cool-weather rains arrive it does need looking after. A rough lawn of mixed grasses still needs to be kept free of weeds with prickly seed capsules if children are to play on it. And such a lawn needs attentive mowing if it is to go into its dormant period in good heart, with reserves of energy ready to make new growth when the season is right. Setting a mower to cut grasses high rather than crop them short is the best way to achieve this and it does seem that rough grasses cut this way do stay greener longer when the months of drought gradually dry up the soil.

If it is decided that some grass is a must, and there can be perfectly good reasons for thinking that, two things must be considered. How much grass is needed and what kind of grasses will be used. Deciding the first is a matter of working out what the grass will be used for, other than to look at — not in itself a good reason for having grass in a garden that bakes dry over summer, and the second decision should be guided by local expertise. Lawn turf and grass seed specialists exist almost everywhere now that golf courses have spread to the furthest corners of the world, or so it seems. Staff in these businesses should be able to advise concerning which mix of grasses will prove reliable in local conditions. The key points to look for are grasses that will grow slowly, make strong, deep root systems and have low water needs. Those grasses which have stoloniferous root systems are most likely to survive drought and return once water is available. Even though some of these have in the past been cried down as too rough, e.g., buffalo grass, Bermuda grass and St Augustine grass, they are far more adaptable and hardy than the fine-leaved grasses of traditional lawns. There is almost continuous research being done on developing new strains of grasses that might be suitable for rough lawns and it is possible to avoid the highly water-dependent varieties which have for so long dominated our thinking.

The advance guard of this movement towards no lawn or less grass uses a whole new language by which to describe their gardening and landscaping activities. For a start 'hard surfaces' and 'soft surfaces' are the new language for the old terms paving, gravel and plants. That is not too hard to absorb I think, but watch out for 'sclerophytes', 'halophytes' and 'xerophytes' among others. So that you can speak with authority when you go to a nursery to buy plants for your 'dry' garden 'sclerophyllous' means, having hard leaves (like an olive tree); 'halophytes' are plants that are able to grow in saline soils and 'xerophytes' are plants that can withstand dry conditions.

Now that the new terminology is in part explained let us consider some of the options other than grass.

When planning to lay out a garden give some thought to what areas of the garden will need to cope with foot traffic, games and outdoor living. According to the household concerned, the areas required for games could be great or nil. Some areas could serve several purposes by using the ground space for both games and outdoor living.

Myrtus communis trained formally

Basketball hoops and other equipment like tables and chairs can be moved out of the way when not required. To cope adequately with the heavy traffic of feet, such areas need hard and durable surfaces, preferably those that drain quickly and wear evenly. The choices range from very expensive cut stone slabs and moderately expensive paving bricks to relatively cheap cement slabs and pavers. How ever they are laid, such materials tend to be rather unremarkable in themselves; the only real variation possible being created by laying the paving in simple patterns, or to have the paving made up with specially cut and fitted pieces which enables a degree of imaginative design. Practicality comes into play too. Who would not want a surface which was as safe as possible for those using it? Flat and evenly laid surfaces, with close, well-fitted paving is essential if trips and falls are to be avoided in areas of heavy use. Breaking up the monotony of large areas of paving such as for basketball, a turning circle, or a crowd of outdoor diners presents a few challenges. It may be possible to draw attention away from the expanse of paving by displaying some particularly attractive potted plants clustered along the margins of the area, or garden furniture may be set out when play has finished. Another option could be to have several large planting boxes or Versailles tubs* standing on bases fitted with castor wheels so that they can easily be moved aside as necessary. Traditionally such tubs have been planted up with standard citrus trees, small palms and cycads, agaves, myrtles, pomegranates and oleanders, but there is plenty of room for using a more diversified range of plants. Likely candidates could be tall aloes, yuccas, frangipani (*Plumeria rubra*), daturas such as *Datura* x 'Golden Queen' or *Datura* x 'Grand Marnier', yesterday, today & tomorrow (*Brunsfelsia latifolia*), night-scented jessamine (*Cestrum nocturnum*), the hummingbird hibiscus (*Hibiscus schizopetalus*) or *Iochroma cyanea* (syn. *I. lanceolata*).

Yucca rostrata,
Huntington
Botanic
Gardens

*caisses de Versailles — this is not pretentious name-dropping; the tubs are constructed so that the sides are demountable, thus allowing dead roots to be trimmed and the soil to be renewed without having to try to tip out the large plants they contain.

Note that not all these plants could be trained to a standard 'lollipop' shape; some, such as the aloes and yuccas have their own distinct silhouettes, while other shrubby plants could have several trunks and half-dome top growth. A truly distinguished garden feature could be made using such potted giants if the were laid out in a formal pattern after the fashion of the garden on the esplanade around Le Lac de la Suisses outside the Orangerie at the palace of Versailles. The scale would naturally have to be somewhat less royal, but even a *corps de ballet* of as few as four tubs could work miracles in an otherwise dull open space. To heighten the impact, some plants could be trimmed as narrow cones; where possible, plants with scented foliage and flowers should be used. Tradition established by the French has the myrtle (*Myrtus communis*) favoured for this role. It is evergreen, the foliage is dark and pleasantly scented when crushed, and the scented white flowers are prolific throughout summer. Myrtle is also amenable to regular trimming. Bay tree (*Laurus nobilis*) is another plant traditionally given this treatment, but there is plenty of choice for experimentation. The shrubby hybrid lantanas could be worth a try, though some may find the scent of the leaves and flowers oppressive, and what about Chinese star jasmine (*Trachelospermum jasminoides*), tree gardenia (*Gardenia thunbergii*) or even the white-flowered plumbago (*Plumbago auriculata* 'Alba'). For contrast, lower-growing shrubs such as the Natal plum (*Carissa macrocarpa*) or lentisc (*Pistacia lentiscus*) could be trained as low-domed shapes. The thing is that the arrangement should be simple, bold and placement regular. Stick to two or three types of plants to achieve the best effect.

The idea may seem at odds with modern thought about casual living, yet within the immense variety of architectural styles now used for home building there are more opportunities for such distinguished arrangements than are taken by home gardeners (who may think such things are either pretentious or too difficult to make). It all depends on the conviction with which the possibilities are exploited. The expense may also seem a big disincentive, especially to those who want instant effects and need therefore to buy everything at once: large tubs, advanced standard trees and shrubs and the paving too, perhaps. Other gardeners with different priorities may well decide to make a beginning with a flexible approach to developing a large paved area where the emphasis may, in the first years, be on the recreation needs of children and young adults; as the years go by and needs change and the focus can move to more decorative designs and experiments with style and with plants. These are other good reasons to plan simply and give it a try by doing the training yourself, even *caisses de Versailles* are not impossible for a reasonable handyperson — I'm not one, but plans are not hard to buy from specialist woodcraft shops. The thing about these things, standard plants and Versailles tubs, is that they last and last. There are trees and tubs at Versailles around 150 years old. Such ancient specimens are obviously beyond the lifetime of any gardener, and may not be high on the wish list of your beneficiaries in any case, but there are really no short cuts. Instant standard trees and cheap pots generally are not going to last, both are frequently produced to stage quick effects and both are likely to be comparatively short-lived. As we are talking here not of following fashion as it changes year by year, but of developing a personal sense of garden style that *may* include some formal features, it is as well to take time, try things out, be able to afford to change them or reject them, and in the end have them well done, or not at all.

And if *caisses de Versailles* are not for you there are always other choices from beautiful terracotta lemon tree pots to serviceable moulded stone reproduction urns to halved wooden wine barrels.

In recent times some landscape designers, drawing from Japanese sources for ideas and plants, have introduced green grass-like plants such as mondo grass (*Ophiopogon japonicus*) set between paving slabs to soften the edges of the hard surfaces. Used between random stone paving or between regularly set rectangular slabs in grid pattern, the low, tufty growth of this evergreen perennial (it's not a grass at all) looks very distinguished. Although not strictly speaking a drought-tolerant plant, mondo grass could be sustained as a useful ground cover in shaded, low traffic areas and look presentable most of the time. With most of their roots sheltered from the heat below the paving slabs and using the moisture that gathers in such places. the plants should survive in Mediterranean-type climates with minimal watering. Mondo grass would not be suitable for large areas, even when used in the ways described, because exposure to bright sun and hot days would cause the leaves to yellow and develop unsightly pale brown scorch marks. Most likely a paving grid design with mondo grass in-fill would be most effectively used in a small, sheltered courtyard with no through traffic. As a background for a centrepiece of sculpture or pottery a setting like this can be highly appropriate.

Should the idea take hold but not the mondo grass, seek alternatives in the small succulent stonecrops (*Sedum* spp.), which should be considerably more tolerant of drought and heat but still appreciating light shade during the hours of fiercest heat. Their leaf coloration could not give the intense, deep green that mondo grass does, but they do give some interesting bronze, yellow and red tones which could be played with to create an imaginative tapestry of colours at ground level, or maybe to pick up the

colours of other parts of the plan. The likes of *Sedum acre, Sedum acre* var. *aureum, Sedum dasyphyllum, Sedum lydium, Sedum spathulifolium* var. *purpurescens* and its silvery-leaved 'Cape Blanco' form as well as the 'Bronze Carpet' and 'Schorbusser Blut' ('Dragon's Blood') forms of *Sedum spurium* all offer distinct possibilities.

In a completely different kind of open bushland garden, large areas of 'soft' hard cover can be achieved very simply by spreading a thick layer of sawdust, small wood chips (sometimes called 'hoggings') or finely shredded pine bark. This will need to be renewed every few years but will provide a safe and flat surface that drains quickly and looks acceptable once it has aged. It is particularly useful under large trees as it does not lift as tree roots grow, nor does it alter the flow of rainwater to the tree roots or change

the drainage patterns of the soil as solid paving materials do. As a precaution against nitrogen starvation to the trees as the mulch begins to break down, it is wise to sprinkle a high nitrogen content fertiliser as these materials are laid. This has an added side benefit in that the fertiliser usually 'ages' the raw whiteness of fresh sawdust and hoggings to an earth-toned grey within a week or so of being spread over the surface and lightly watered in. Be very cautious with the fertiliser lest the trees be damaged by the increased levels of nitrogen. Let emphasis be placed on 'sprinkle'.

Such paving methods are now very common in children's playgrounds where

they provide a durable soft landing surface for slides and swings. With some thoughtful planning and good background planting these materials can be a very presentable ground cover. They are especially suited to gardens that have been made within remnants of forest or bushland as the materials blend well with the leaf and twig litter that accumulates naturally.

It is as well to recognise that shredded bark, sawdust and hogged wood chips have at least two disadvantages: they can add to the fire risk of some properties, and they can be fouled by dogs and cats. Preventive measures should include regular raking

Aloe arborescens gives cold-weather cheer to gardens, and to honey-eating birds.

1
3
5

and picking up of twig and leaf litter and a means of damping down the area by fitting up a system of mini-jet sprinklers that can be turned on as needed. A surprise drenching may serve to discourage pets using the area as a toilet; otherwise immediate removal of their mess as needed will have to be the order of the day. Pet training to overcome the problem may be possible and, of course, there may be other acts of discouragement, but I wouldn't know anything about them, would I?

In many old gardens of Provence, Spain, Italy and Greece a deep layer of sand is often used as the paving material. It works well, provided the stuff can be tolerated indoors too! Like the products mentioned, above it is a 'soft' hard surface and does require some regular care and maintenance, but it has the advantages of being relatively cheap, widely available and long-lasting. And it usually has neutral colour tones which effectively set off surrounding greenery. Because it is very finely textured, it can be raked into pleasing patterns and if kept flat, shows up the patterns cast by shadows very well.

Also seen in old gardens are river-worn stones set out to make a cobblestone paving, or in mosaic patterns picked out by pebbles of the same colour. In European gardens these may feature striking heraldic devices or elaborate Rococo curlicues while in old Chinese gardens the patterns are most often repeated carpet-like and feature simplified floral motifs or geometric designs. Such things are delightful but are they possible today? So many regions now prohibit the gathering of natural resources such as river-worn pebbles and boulders. Wherever possible items such as cobbles and stone setts (often found in stable yards) should be recycled from old gardens as should redundant street paving stones and old kerbstones which can find a new life as components of garden paths. If it is possible to obtain river-washed stones, or those from shingle beaches, good use can be made of them.

In areas away from heavy traffic hard paving can be much more varied and exciting than paving bricks, cut stone and cement slabs; even those laid in patterns. The creativity of individual gardeners can really be given a much freer hand so long as the path remains accessible and safe to use in all weathers.

The best and most charming informal effects can be achieved by laying such paths with an amateur's whimsical eye. Where precision laying and engineered flatness are not required a gardener may choose to take on the task and bring to it such imaginative combinations as occur when possible paving materials and inspiration come together. Describing such possibilities in nigh impossible for who may know what may inspire a gardener cum paviour to put two, three or more kinds of stuff together? As general guides, remember that new and recycled materials can be combined most effectively, and that different kinds of paving can serve to link and define different parts of a garden. In the first instance, cement paving slabs (turned upside down for better footing) could be combined with almost any other durable material to build a pattern. During the 18th century all manner of bizarre things were used for making patterned paving — knuckle bones, large teeth from horses and cows, fossils and geological specimens. It would be hard to obtain such things today, though I have seen French paving stones patterned like ammonite fossils. Most likely gardeners of today will be able to reuse broken cement slabs, broken pots, pebbles, old terracotta roof tiles or drain tiles, old bricks and pieces of old bricks, and stones graded by size or colour with which to create interesting paved paths. Taking the idea one step further and to the second suggestion, a path such as the one described could change when it arrives at a particular part of a garden where it is hoped visitors will pause to observe some small feature such a water-filled garden pot on which a flower may be floated. The usual paving pattern giving way to a different surface, perhaps broadening out into a small clearing overhung with shrubs and displaying a fine piece of pottery or a whimsical driftwood sculpture. Moving on, the path resumes its previous combination of materials and pattern. In designs such as this it is not necessary, as it would be in a formal design for such 'incidents' as the pottery or sculpture to be visible at a distance and act as an eye-catcher. The path serves to draw people down itself and into the garden. This understanding allows such objects to be revealed more informally, placed on the paving but partly concealed by growth or set aside in the garden among the plants.

Thus far I have refrained from any commentary on crazy paving; that paving made up from flat pieces of random slate or sandstone that has had several periods of vogue in the last hundred years, mainly in the various cottage garden revivals and the fashions for rustic adornments to gardens. It is much overdone, being left over from gardens laid out in the 1940s. To my way of thinking it is best when sparingly used and combined with other paving to make a diverting composition. Thus there might be stretches of crazy paving running through the garden but interrupted with an area of solid paving blocks with a small piece of pottery used as a bird bath, and the changes of level in the path marked by large stone risers set across it at right angles. At the lowest level, furthest from the strong architectural lines of the house, the stone paving may give way to a path cut from rough grass through a copse of hardy shrubs. Used this way, with no grass between the stones, the fiddly work of keeping the grass trim is eliminated. The bare earth could be colonised with small hardy bulbs; I've seen one

example where tiny *Cyclamen coum* 'Album' and several kinds of *Crocus speciosus* have seeded themselves into cracks in crazy paving where no human hand could ever persuade them to grow. The soil is thick with the roots of nearby shrubs and bone dry in summer and yet the wee plants thrive.

Whether setting cobblestones or mixed paving, or crazy paving in place it must be settled firmly into some sort of bedding. Cement is unnecessary and ugly, and prevents any happy incidental plant growth. However, good results can be obtained with coarse builders sand, unwashed and with the 'fines' capable of setting fairly hard once it is dry. This unpromising looking stuff does not seem to deter volunteer seedlings and is easily disguised by the natural establishment of mosses and other minute growths. To start a base of sand must be laid flat and deep enough to bed the stones or bricks

Limestone cobbles in rough winter grass

to about half their depth; next it should be rolled and watered lightly so that the base is settled and well consolidated. Once this surface has had a chance to dry out partially, laying the bricks or stones can begin. Bricks are easiest so long as care is taken to ensure even spacing between each brick and a flat upper surface. Not all bricks are exactly the same so a little excavation or backfilling may be needed to accommodate minor imperfections. Stones and cobbles and broken bits and pieces need more care but the principle is the same. A hint concerning cobbles and other water-rounded stones; they will be most firmly set if they are positioned upright on their narrowest edge. When the stones or other materials are in position dry sand should be dribbled around them and swept firmly into place with a stiff-bristled yard broom; some banging and tapping to make sure all the gaps are filled is allowed, though not so hard that the stones are dislodged. It is best to work one section at a time, rather than try to do a complete job

in one go, working slowly and ensuring
that the materials are as firmly set as
possible. The next step is to sprinkle the
completed section with a hose to further
compact and settle the sand infill. If gaps
appear these can be refilled with more
dry sand. An overall top-up might be
necessary and then a further brooming
off and damping down. Once the sand
has dried thoroughly the whole surface
can be swept briskly to remove any
excess sand. The stones should be well
set and safe to walk on. Should builders
sand not be available with fines included
a mix of sand and cement could be used;
mixing proportions are difficult to gauge

ABOVE:

*Random stone
paving,
Pomona,
California*

LEFT:

*Inexpensive
Thai pots filled
with annuals
provide spot
colour on a
brick-paved
terrace.*

1
3
9

but about eight of sand to one of cement ought to be sufficient and not too impenetrable to the roots of volunteer seedlings when it has dried.

It might be as well at this point to understand the difference between landscaping and gardening. The two terms are much used interchangeably and the differences are quite distinct; though it is possible to start out with either and gradually develop into the other by a process of adding more or taking things away. Both are activities related to ornamental and environmental horticulture, and as far as we are concerned in these pages are to do with the development of domestic surroundings. Landscaping the grounds of a home most often is a once only event with everything done that needs to be done to set up an appearance and environment tailored to meet the particular needs and lifestyle of the inhabitants. When all is done the household can get on with what pursuits interest them most. The 'garden' around the house is not a major focus of their lives and keeping it in good order is simply another part of the necessary housework. Gardening is an altogether more personal interest and pursuit that does occupy a significant part of some people's leisure time and is a hobby and recreation much the same as wind-surfing, floral art, gambling or opera-going. It tends to be developmental; growing, changing focus and perhaps becoming highly specialised as the years go by. It is engrossing and time-consuming. The intensity with which it is pursued can vary from gardener to gardener, and within a gardener's lifetime. It can be undertaken at great expense or done very cheaply. It can be a solitary pleasure or done for the pleasure of others and it always involves direct contact with the soil, resting, planning and planting in accord with the rhythm of the seasons, and making a response — sympathetic, or otherwise — to the environment in which the garden is made.

When it comes to 'soft surfaces' in a garden, that is the plants with which a garden is furnished, the differences between landscaping and gardening can be fairly evident. A landscaped garden will most likely be composed of very few varieties of plants used in large numbers to cover the soil with greenery that will require minimal maintenance. It is common enough for landscaped gardens to be covered with a great masses of African daisy (*Osteospermum eklonis*), *Myoporum parvifolium* and the rosy ice plant (*Drosanthemum floribundum*). A feature planting of the various forms of *Ceanothus griseus* var. *horizontalis* could appear along with a bank of *Cistus* hybrids — for a bit of colour. The background may be made up with dense plantations of *Correa alba*, *Grevillea thelemanniana* and *Westringia fruticosa* and a few gum trees; the likes of *Eucalyptus cinerea*, *E. perriniana* or *E. pulverulenta*. With luck there might be a yucca to add a touch of interest, and without doubt there will be several clumps of artistically deployed boulders. An easy care

1
4
0

garden, all it needs is a quick once over every month and then its back to the golf course; a landscape for leisure if ever there was one. More than likely the landscape will stay more or less the same until the owners sell up and move on, or until some major construction work on the house provides an opportunity for a landscape update. Serviceable, yes but boring too — at least as far as this gardener goes. There are just so many more possibilities, even for those who buy a landscaped garden. And for those who are gardeners, or those who may eventually become gardeners the chapters of this book offer a glimpse of the diversity and beauty that can be achieved with a little effort and imagination in climates that are warm and dry in summer.

PATTERNS OF
black &
green

Casting around for the means of introducing my theme here, I skimmed the pages of a good many of the old classics on gardening in Mediterranean climates and those areas having summers that are long, hot and dry. Mrs Martineau (Gardening in Sunny Lands) *didn't appear to have much to say on the subject of the basic elements of shade and greenery so important to our purpose.*

Rose Standish Nichols (*Spanish and Portuguese Gardens*) had some inspiring illustrations but seemed not to have given much thought to why such things as these would be important while Pliny's separate letters to his friends Gallus and Apollinaris showed he fully understood why shade and greenery were important in Roman gardens but somehow he didn't quite carry his observations far enough. Observant, and sometimes witty Helen Morgenthau Fox (*Patio Gardens*) made an inspirational study of

Previous pages:

*(p. 142) From
shadow into
light—the
White Garden,
Sissinghurst
Castle*

*(p. 143)
Euphorbia
characias cv
'Burrow Silver'*

garden making that sought to translate the traditions of Moorish Spain to the glittering social colonies of Los Angeles and San Francisco, but stuck mainly to the decorative items needed to compose Spanish gardens as set pieces. Edith Wharton (*Italian Villas and their Gardens*) had a bit to say that hints at the theme; at least she understood that the impact of dark shadows and the myriad shades of green created much more than a picture. It is the *sensation*, the feeling of the transition from light to shade that is important. Moving from one to the other makes us feel refreshed. The hundreds of shades of green from almost black and deepest jade to pale acid greens also add another layer of sensation, that of serenity and inner calm which adds to the relief offered by gardens in a sun-steeped climate.

Still these few brief references cannot be all there is on the nuances of shadow and greenery. Perhaps I should have consulted Constance Villiers Stuart (*Gardens of the Great Mughals*) but by purest chance I happened instead on a very slim volume titled *Passenger to Teheran* by Victoria Sackville-West. It is a kind of travelogue but it goes someway beyond mere descriptions and demonstrates in part a profound understanding of the fitness of gardens to their surroundings; an idea which the author later developed with rare facility in her famous garden at Sissinghurst Castle.

'Garden?' we say; and think of lawns and herbaceous borders, which is manifestly absurd. There is no turf in this arid country; and as for herbaceous borders they postulate a lush shapeliness unimaginable to the Persian mind. Here, everything is dry and untidy, crumbling and decayed; a dusty poverty exposed for eight months of the year to a cruel sun. For all that, there are gardens in Persia. But they are gardens of trees, not of flowers; green wildernesses. Imagine that you have ridden for four days across a plain; that you have then come to a barrier of snow mountains and ridden up the pass; that from the top of the pass you have seen a second barrier of mountains in the distance, a hundred miles away; that you know beyond these mountains lies yet another plain, and another, and another; and that for days, even weeks, you must ride, with no shade, and the sun overhead, and nothing but the bleached bones of dead animals strewing the track. Then when you come to trees and running water, you will call it a garden. It will not be flowers and their garishness that your eyes crave for, but a green cavern full of shadow, and pools where goldfish dart, and the sound of the little streams. That is the meaning of a garden in Persia.

That was long ago and far away; who knows what Vita Sackville-West would have made out of opportunities to garden in a warm, dry climate? At least she appears to have responded to the sensations roused by such climates; to have understood the impact on the human spirit of heat and drought and glaring sunlight, and to appreciate how different is the meaning of gardens and the sense of place that develops in such an

Drawing the garden visitor deeper into the garden the patches of sunlight showing the way, Hidcote Manor

environment. And that is what we must do too, if we are to garden well and happily in the places where we live far removed from the soft light, gentle climate and well-watered gardens where herbaceous borders find a home.

That is not to say that we cannot learn useful lessons from gardens and gardeners nurtured in climates more benign than those we share. One important lesson that will greatly assist our acclimatisation is to learn to understand the value of green as a colour

1
4
5

in our gardens. If as I have suggested the garden in summer is to be one of repose and quietude in sympathy with the suspended state of growth of the natural vegetation, green as a colour takes on prime importance. Not, mind you, that everything must be green. The grass of lawns and orchards and walks will be as scrawny, dry and bleached as any hay field or summer pasture, but that can be very acceptable so long as other plants retain their green mantle and create that feeling of coolness so necessary to relieve the overpowering fatigue of the heat. (Dry grass in lawns and paths looks the better if it is not pocked with the ever green rosettes of dandelions.)

Indeed, such a pallid foreground can be a very telling foil for a varied range of greens, and the variety can be added to by the inclusion of plants with leaves of different textures from dull and rugose to glossy and smooth. Among my favourites, and also among the most reliable plants are salvias. Tall, erect growth and dark green, rough leaves are found in *Salvia guaranitica*. The short spikes of cobalt blue flowers generally appear in autumn but at this season the two-metre high growth makes a solid screen of close-packed stems and dense foliage. This contrasts well with almost any other form of foliage. Large clumps of *Iris spuria* hybrids with tall, narrow leaves look good in front along with a bold dome-shaped mass of *Salvia dorisiana*. In this salvia the leaves are approximately the same shape as the leaves of an apricot tree; pale acid green in colour and hairy; they are also deliciously scented with a perfume redolent of grapefruit. There are other choices that could be used instead of the spuria irises; *Iris demetrii* is one that I specially like the look of — fine upright leaves of a greenish-blue that lasts all summer long. The stiff and slightly arched leaves of *Dietes iridioides* or *D. bicolor* would work just as well, and the somewhat taller *Aristea major* (syn. *A. thyrsiflora*) is also a candidate to contrast with the other foliage forms. A last option could be *Dietes robinsoniana* which has all the stature of New Zealand flax (*Phormium tenax*) with equally bold, simple leaves and tall spikes of large creamy white 'butterfly' blooms. But maybe I am getting ahead of myself with such detail. It seems that other, more important aspects of the greenness of things have been skimmed over too quickly.

What moderate-sized trees can provide an attractive background of greenery to see our gardens through those long, hot months of summer? Bearing in mind always that the choice of trees must be very carefully made in order to ensure that the conditions of the site will suit the tree chosen my consideration would be focussed on achieving shady areas under spreading trees, using trees to create some screening from unsightly buildings and to give privacy, and to have variety of shape. Spreading shade trees suited to suburban gardens include the cultivated forms of *Gleditsia triacanthos* such

1
4
6

as 'Sunshine' and 'Burgundy Lace', *Koelreuteria paniculata, Aesculus californica, Ginkgo biloba*. Note that these are all deciduous trees and thus would allow winter sunshine to warm the house and gardens that fall under their summertime shadows. Evergreen trees of a more upright habit are most valuable for screening suburban gardens from outside vantage points and for planting along boundary lines. *Acacia pendula, Casuarina stricta, Eucalyptus sideroxylon* 'Rosea', *Tamarix aphylla* are popular choices but there are many more to be found listed in publications such as *Landscape Plants for Western Regions* by Bob Perry. There are many possibilities in plant families yet barely introduced to gardeners, especially among the oaks of California, Turkey and the Mediterranean region. The madrone (*Arbutus menziesii*), the manzanitas (*Arctostaphyllos* spp.), the Mt Etna broom (*Genista aetnensis*) and the multi-trunked mallees (*Eucalyptus* spp.) offer more choices as do the acacias from the south-western states of the United States and Australia (*Acacia farnesiana, A. densiflora* and *A. stenophylla*) and then there are palms to consider too. *Butia capitata*, now there is a palm of exciting beauty; such beautiful blue-grey leaves. How stunning they would look planted in a grove in front of *Tamarix aphylla* and surrounded with blue-grey agaves and underplanted with mats of *Senecio mandraliscae* and rosettes of *Echeveria secunda*. Maybe a fountain or two of *Festuca amethystina* to spark up the composition — a song in silver. Perhaps the massive lumps of furnace glass, gleaming and pallid blue that were deployed by Mme Ganna Walska around her 'blue' garden at Lotusland, Santa Barbara in California would be going too far. Yes, clearly that would be too much. There I go again, getting led astray by the association of heady ideas.

What small trees have leaves that are both interesting and exhibit varied tones of green? Carob tree (*Ceratonia siliqua*), pomegranate (*Punica granatum*), especially. *P. g.* 'Madame Legrelle' with coral red flowers edges in creamy white, pineapple guava (*Feijoa sellowiana*), wilga (*Geijera parviflora*), bay tree (*Laurus nobilis*), mountain pine (*Pinus mugo*) ...all answer the call. Apart from the distinctive leaf attributes of each, they all can be grown as small trees with multiple trunks free of branches up to 2.5 m clear of the ground. 'Limbed up' this way the tree-like nature of the plants is enhanced and the space underneath can become another place to garden creatively. If the shade cast by these trees is too dense for plants to thrive it is possible to thin the canopy of the tree by judiciously removing a few branches of leafy growth. The shady area under these evergreen trees is usually deep and dark; on the hottest days the shaded areas will appear black and cool. Such caverns of shadow are quickly populated with sleeping cats and children quietly making cubby holes; a sure sign that these spots are most useful in hot, sunny weather. Aside from their usefulness as places that are sheltered and cool,

1

4

7

ABOVE: Dietes Robinsoniana, *the Lord Howe Island wedding iris reaches two metres at flowering time.*

RIGHT: *Pines offer a wide variety of habit, evergreen foliage and interesting cone shapes—* Pinus wallichiana.

these 'black holes' are important visually in giving a garden depth. Under the intense sunlight of high summer, everything in view tends to bleach into one shallow plane in the flash and glare outdoors; the depth of shadows tends to overcome this flattening effect. If the shadows can play across a flat surface such as a gravelled court the visual impression will be one of a deeper perspective, and there will be the added bonus of stark contrasts in patterns of black on the gravel. Think how the shadow cast by a sculpture, elaborate pot or a tree with an interestingly shaped trunk could add an almost theatrical feeling to a simple garden space. Of course siting the object and the space in relation to the sun would be important, but the critical part would be amusing: the selection of the object that would throw the shadow; now imagining how that would work would be a challenge.

Another interesting picture based on dark shadows and bright light can be made by so arranging things that a view to a garden can be seen under and through a darkened space such as might be made by a tree or arcade. Now the easy part is to organise a tree through which to look to a distant garden or scene that might well be further framed by dense plantings beyond the tree; the harder part is to find such possibilities in a piece of building. With all the work that goes on these days constructing breezeways, pavilions, colonnades, cloisters, gazebos and suntraps near swimming pools maybe the idea could be given a workout? The possibility of sitting on a lightly shaded patio looking through a darkened space onto a swimming pool, sun bright and dazzling is, well, dazzling. How much more dramatic if a specimen of *Dracaena draco, Aloe plicatilis, Euphorbia ingens* or *Beaucarnea recurvata* (syn. *Nolina recurvata*) is displayed in a large tub set against a wall to terminate the view ? What colour could the wall be; cobalt blue, dark terracotta, white rough cast adobe, or perhaps a soft sandy colour?

The dramatic flower buds of Dietes Robinsoniana

The idea of having a 'window' into a garden from one part to another is not new, yet all too infrequently seen, especially in modern gardens where open plan landscaping allows everything to be seen at once, or where cottage garden cuteness precludes any construction more solid than a dovecote. But here and there the old idea resurfaces, perhaps as a garden gate set in a wall or wall with a decorative wrought iron screen or

1
4
9

grille set into it. These were popular in the 1920s and 1930s in Spanish Mission style homes; a few were included in the walled terraces of some Art Deco houses and even later Cubist and Modernist style houses sometimes had porthole type windows built into garden walls. Has the idea been explored by Post-Modern architects? The possibilities seem pretty exciting considering the broken wall and industrial ruin style markers that seem to be almost trademarks on new buildings everywhere.

The most important considerations in having a garden window are that there must be something to see, and there must be a focus on the hole-in-the-wall with few other distracting objects in sight, so that attention is directed at the window and the curiosity aroused to look through it to the other side. From the vantage point of a terrace or patio, the wall should be comparatively blank while on the other side lush or dramatic foliage, rocks or a water feature may be seen through the window. There is nothing like wanting to see what is on the other side to raise the levels of anticipation and increase sensations. So much the better then to strike through the heat of midsummer with a view from a sunny courtyard into a garden of darkest greens and deep shadows.

Having already given some thought to small evergreen trees, let us see what deciduous small trees have foliage of sufficient strength and interest to carry them through the hot, dry season? Palo verde (*Caesalpinia praecox*), weeping silver-leaf pear (*Pyrus salicifolia 'Pendula'*), ocotillo (*Fouquieria splendens*), Russian olive (*Elaeagnus angustifolia*), western redbud (*Cercis occidentalis*) — a brief selection that offers some exciting potential.

But the fun part really comes about when looking for plants for the foreground. Here the lively qualities of greenery can come fully into play. Big bold plants such as agaves and aloes come in more shades of green than those with silver-grey farinas dusted over their leaves; these are found in the common sorts such as *Agave americana* and *Aloe plicatilis*, but there are many others to choose from e.g., *Agave shawii*, *Agave victoriae-reginae* and *Aloe nobilis*. These will tolerate really arid conditions during the hottest months so long as their succulent leaves are well-charged with water stored from the rainy months. There are many other plants that will perform perfectly well given some occasional water and good mulching to keep the soil cool and so reduce evaporation. I have already spoken with some enthusiasm for salvias. By good fortune more and more species are being introduced to our gardens via enthusiastic study groups, private collections in the field in Mexico and central America and by an increasing number of nurseries alert to the possibilities salvias offer. In complete contrast, I find that in my own environment tree peonies add a touch of foliate drama during the hot months. These have been raised from seed received from botanic gardens as far afield as St Petersburg and Vladivostok. The seedlings begin to flower after about five years and by that time are sufficiently well-established in my garden to need no water through the hot season other than what may come by way of very infrequent thunder storms. Many people find this rather surprising as tree peonies have a certain reputation for being difficult. I find they are not half so difficult as their herbaceous cousins. Once their very stout root systems are well-developed, the plants are very hardy, provided they are grown where no tree roots compete for the available moisture. I mulch heavily with a very loose blanket of straw and shredded tree prunings and that seems to do the trick in my situation. The plants are fully exposed to the heat of the afternoon sun and are planted in a deep, though shaly loam. During the hottest weeks of the hot months we get day temperatures of around (and over) 40° Celsius. Sometimes it pays to be adventurous and experiment with plants! The key information to remember in trying such an idea is to look for plants that have strong, stout root systems that suggest in themselves the possibility to go deep into the soil to seek and store water. The other critical factor is that the plants should be finished their annual growth spurt and flowering well before the hot season arrives. In the case of tree peonies some slight chill may be needed also to trigger flower formation. In this garden, very light frosts are experienced for a few weeks in the depths of the cold season.

So when the hot weather arrives tall growth and striking foliage of the tree peonies remain to add a note of distinction to the several parts of the garden where they grow.

But maybe these beauties are not adapted to other sites and slightly different climates. Does that mean a kind of horticultural boredom is imposed by visual sameness and lack-lustre leafage? Of course not; it is a matter of looking about and finding things that will grow and are interesting to look at when they are not in flower. Things that come readily to mind are a trio of plants rarely seen though they have been around for a long time and were reasonably well known to 19th century gardeners who toiled in the places where we now live. I refer to *Montanoa bipinnatifida*, *Wigandia caracasana* and *Bocconia arborea*.

Now there are three tough plants. And there are three plants with astonishingly good foliage; foliage that is big, bold and bountiful. The montanoa has noble leaves, deeply divided into pointed divisions and towering heads of white daisies in autumn. The wigandia has large dark green leaves rather like a violin in outline and rich blue flowers after the style of a large forget-me-not. Growth is tall and shrubby. Other

woody, shrubby plants that are very tough are the mahonias, especially the species which come from the west coast of North America. It is to be regretted that these fine plants are not so widely available as they could be. This may arise from their not being regarded as first-rank plants by the leaders of garden fashion in England and Europe, however they should be sought out whenever an opportunity makes it possible to obtain them. Oregon grape (*Mahonia aquifolium*) is perhaps the most widely known but there are also *M. nevinii* and California grape (*M. pinnata*) and the prostrate *M. repens.* Then again the various forms of the tree dahlia are also fairly impressive in stature, flower production and leaves that are distinctive. Besides the common lavender pink form (*Dahlia imperialis*) there are also a reddish pink form (*D. imperialis* 'Coccinea'), a single white form and a double white form. There may well be

The sunlight at the end of the dark shadowy tunnel cast by this holm oak (Quercus ilex) serves to focus our attention on the gateway beyond.

others too; at least one other form was recorded in the 19th century — a variety with pale pink to white flowers with darker pink tones at the centre of each flower, and there may yet be other varieties developed by plant breeders interested in exploring the potential of this hardy plant.

Yet flowering shrubby perennials such as these may be too demanding of water to be planted by some garden makers. In this case greater use must be made of the many other genera that are drought-tolerant. The dozens of species of euphorbia are a good example of a very adaptable clan, though they are generally intolerant of frost and poorly drained soils. Besides the large tree forms (*Euphorbia ingens* and *E. coopperii*) discussed earlier, there are a number of excellent soft-wooded shrubby forms that are often regarded as evergreen perennials. In the main these make more or less dome-shaped mounds of green or grey-green leaves and stems: *Euphorbia mellifera, E. dendroides,*

1
5
2

E. characias, E. characias subsp. *'Wulfennii', E. rigida,* and *E. cyparissias.* There are many other euphorbias more succulent than these and thereby more drought-tolerant e.g., *Euphorbia tirucallii, E. milii* (crown of thorns), *E. canariensis* and *E. resinifera,* but these have habits of growth which render them more useful as plants to make a statement with and to act as exclamation points in a garden than for mass planting.

More drought-resistant still than euphorbias are the mat-forming evergreen succulent plants that are available. Most drought-tolerant of all are the mesembryanthemums, often called ice plant or pigface and capable of forming dense mats of foliage and trailing stems. Now the names of these seem to change quite remarkably according to which botanical point of view is holding sway at the time. While the plants as a family are commonly known by all three names above, their generic name can be *Meleophora, Delosperma* or *Lampranthus* depending on which particular plant is being described! Quite often they are found in nurseries simply grouped by flower colour — red, pink, yellow, orange, white, lilac pink and wine red. Where these plants are massed the overall impact of the garden can be heightened by planting something altogether bigger to rise out of the mat of ground hugging foliage. Yuccas, agaves,

aloes, and tall euphorbias (*Euphorbia grandicornis, E. pseudocactus, E. neriifolia, E. candelabrum*) could be placed to advantage. When the plants are not in flower the contrast of shape, habits of growth and the variety of greens in leaves and stems will be ample to carry interest through the hottest weather.

A rustic garden seat in a shady corner makes a pleasant retreat.

More definitely perennial in their manner of growth and blessed with foliage that has strong architectural qualities are *Ferula communis, Crambe cordifolia* and *Acanthus mollis* that have been mentioned before. There are other plants from the same families

1
5
3

which suggest themselves as likely candidates for inclusion in a dry, Mediterranean style garden. A great set of source books are found in Roger Phillips and Martyn Rix *Perennials*, (Vols 1 and 2) and from them a few others from these families recommend themselves: *Crambe maritima, Acanthus dioscoridis, A. syriacus, A. longifolius* while *Ferula kuhistanica* may yet prove useful too. Other plants whose presence suggests that they have a part to play in a green symphony are the more statuesque eryngiums — *Eryngium variifolium, E. maritimum, E. lasseauxii* (syn. *E. pandanifolium*) and *E. bourgatii*. I have also tried *E. campestre* and *E. leavenworthii* and found them worthwhile in flower and foliage. These plants, like many others grow well in soils that are well-drained and like many plants that self-sow freely they tend to appear in greatest numbers in gravelly paths and in cracks between paving stones; not always the most useful positions but extracted at the four-leaf stage such seedlings transplant readily to the places they are wanted.

Another group of plants that are remarkably adaptable are the species of clematis and their near hybrids. In particular, the non-climbing (scandent) forms are worth trying out. In the main they must be raised from seeds as they are not much grown in the nursery trade, but then isn't that part of the fun of gardening? I am still experimenting myself but have found *Clematis recta* 'Purpurea', *C.* x 'Jouniana' and *C.* x 'Jouniana Praecox' available from nurseries and quite useful as sprawling ground-covers with attractive green mantles of leaves; their flowers tend to be rather non-descript — modest could be regarded as generous by those accustomed to the larger glories of 'Lasurstern' and 'Aumann'. *Clematis recta* 'Purpurea' has dark purplish foliage and stems with small starry white flowers and the other pair have pale blue bells half-hidden among the foliage and tangle of trailing stems. These last two are vigorous and can cover an area of 2 m² with one season's growth. Hard pruning is advocated to obtain a dense cover of leaves with no bare stems exposed. I am still experimenting with a good many other clematis including *Clematis freemontii, C. addisonii* and *C. integrifolia*. One other clematis is worth looking out for is *C.* x *bonstedtii* 'Wyvale' — the bell-shaped flowers are a telling shade of blue and the large divided leaves on shrubby stems are a good contrast with the heavy fountains of greenery produced by hybrid *Hemerocallis* (day lilies) and with the stiffer fans of *Aristea caerulea* and *Libertia grandiflora*.

Those accustomed to gardening in climates where summers are long, hot and dry will have already been greatly surprised by my assertions about the value of tree peonies in such conditions. By happenstance I find that other correspondents from the world of gardeners also find that these plants are much tougher than European authorities lead us to believe through their experience.

1
5
4

It is not my intention to get into detailed descriptions of species and varieties here; there are other books such as the two volumes mentioned above that do that task rather well. What I do want to do is suggest that there are plenty of plants hardy in warm dry climates that have attractive, interesting and drought-resistant foliage that are capable of maintaining strong visual interest in a garden throughout the hot, summer months. They are quite able to carry the garden through a period of what otherwise can be regarded as the hot weather doldrums. Even without having many flowers a garden can be green and glorious.

native

DIVERSIONS

AND OTHER PROBLEMS

Having taken an interest for some years in the garden history of places like Australia, California and the Cape of Good Hope, I think I can discern a broadly similar pattern of appreciation for the plants native to those areas. I would not make any claim for distinguished study in the area, but simply observe a few similarities.

First arrivals in any new settlement – Sydney Cove, San Diego de Alcala or Cape Town had as their horticultural priority the provision of fresh food. Gardens which could survive were critical to the success of any colonial venture; resupply from established settlements, or from home bases in Europe was not reliable and a degree of independence was therefore a great urgency as starvation was never far away if relief ships carrying provisions failed to arrive on time. Settlements were made for reasons that often had more to do with military, political and religious considerations than with

Previous pages:

(p. 156) One of

the most

attractive

Australian

native plants—

Banksia

serrata

(p. 157)

Leucospermum

nutans

an accurate appraisal of the potential of the site chosen. Thus it was that such places were described by their proponents in glowing terms that were all too quickly proven inaccurate, if not downright misleading. Lush pastures, reliable water supplies, friendly natives and rich farmland mostly turned out to be nothing of the kind. Coping with the hardships generated as a result of the mismatch between expectations and reality was made doubly difficult because very few of the first settlers had much agricultural or farming knowledge, and most importantly none had any knowledge of the prevailing weather patterns in the new settlements. The years taken to build up an understanding of the pattern of the seasons were years of hardship and hunger. Exploration took place to determine what resources of the settled lands might usefully add to the wealth of the colonising powers, but the collection of mineralogical, zoological and botanical specimens had more impact in the academic centres of Europe than it did on the daily struggles of those first colonists. Individuals did collect specimens and send them back to patrons and institutions in Europe, but these were most often private and personal activities, albeit condoned and sometimes supported at official levels. Specimens reaching scientists in Europe were described, classified and illustrated and most often considered to be the property of the monarch from whose territory they had been collected. So it was that specimens came to be housed in royal collections — in archives, cabinets, galleries and gardens where they were on view to the aristocrats who attended court. By this influence arose vogues among the nobility to form their own collections of this and that; some even sponsored their own collectors and thereby the fashion (and supply of specimens) was passed down to the admiring lesser orders of society. It was by this means that matters botanical and horticultural became the province of amateurs, especially during the 19th century.

Eventually colonial life became more secure in the new lands, reliable patterns of husbandry and agriculture developed and there was some time for more leisurely pursuits. At this stage of development it seems that there occurred a unique combination of fashion and circumstances which saw a strong interest in collecting and growing native plants wherever people had settled. We would not admire the ruthless collection methods that were practised; entire populations of desirable bulbs, ferns, orchids, alpines and succulents were stripped from their environments and sold wholesale. The loss rates must have been extremely high but such was the attitude of the times that this was often considered an advantage commercially as it vastly inflated the value of those plants that did survive. Naturally, those people who enjoyed gardening as a pastime in the colonies were close to the sources of the plants most desired by European collectors. The irony of amateurs in the backwaters of the colonies growing plants in the open air that could only be grown in the heated glass 'stoves' of the nobility in Europe was not lost on the horticulturalists of the day. Nor is it now; there are many interesting commentaries among the books that trace the various colonial garden histories.

With gardens chock full of transplanted specimens it would be thought that gardeners of those early days would have been agog with excitement and bursting with pride. And they were — for a while. But fashions changed as they always do, and horticultural one-upmanship moved on to new vogues; the mania for collecting things, sometimes called 'museumism', gave way to a passion for landscaping, for arranging things and composing picturesque garden effects with plants. And something else happened which has not been much written about: colonial gardeners found that many native plants did not respond well to active gardening; native plants did not flourish under the traditional regimen of digging, fertilising, pruning, training, intense planting, heavy watering and rearranging. The sense of frustration that must surely have developed as result of this conflict of keen interest and a poorly understood reality no doubt disillusioned many colonial gardeners keen to grow native plants in all their variety. The psychology of denial possibly came into play; gardeners knew they were doing all the right things in terms of garden work and yet found that native plants failed to thrive. If the methods of gardening were 'right' (i.e., gardening according to established knowledge) and the plants did not grow, then it must have been that the plants were 'wrong'. This was a powerful disincentive that still pervades the experience and attitudes of many gardeners who attempt to grow native plants without knowledge or consideration of their cultural requirements today. Many native plants were also found to be short-lived and grew increasingly ugly as they collapsed into old age; a good many also required special conditions for germination and vigorous growth — all matters which were hardly understood by gardeners of the times. The fascination with native plants waned quickly and was supplanted with new fashions for making picturesque and Romantic landscapes. Native plants were largely ignored as gardeners sought to recreate the new wave of styles from Europe.

Another wave of enthusiasm for native plants appears to have occurred when the flora had been more fully explored and 'garden worthy', decorative plants identified from the bulk of less spectacular species. While it is not possible here to detail when this development occurred in each of the countries concerned, it does appear to have had links with a developing sense of national or regional identity, and to have generated

1

5

9

*Leucodendron
x 'Silvan Red'
is but one of
many colourful
hybrids of this
beautiful South
African genus.*

a wider debate about maintaining roadside vegetation, preserving tracts of bushland and forest as well as including native plants in gardens that were 'truly' Australian, 'genuinely' South African or a 'real' reflection of the Golden State, California.

A third wave of enthusiasm is discernible too, which is swirling about us now; perhaps not with the same rush and swash as previously, but none-the-less quietly pervasive and spreading further afield. The enthusiasm has found expression in a greater depth of understanding about how native plants grow and increase, and the conditions and associations which they need to flourish. Those gardeners who have mastered the cultivation of native plants have gone further and begun to develop new hybrids — look at the numerous examples found in grevillea, leucodendron, protea and ceanothus. With cultural requirements better understood and publicised, and with exciting 'new' natives available, gardeners are once again trying them. The marketing people have been at work too, and native plants are now mostly sold not on their 'native' image but by their garden worthiness, by their hardiness, by their colourful displays and by their capacity for 'integration' in a typical garden of mixed shrubs and flowers. Unlike other periods when native plants were popular, this time round, instead of simply collecting plants people are now far more interested in using native plants to give expression to ideas from other parts of the world. In particular, they are now able to use the wide range of native plants and their hybrids to create gardens based on a colour theme; blue, white and yellow gardens are as possible with plants native to one of our regions as it would with the traditional highly bred and selected garden flowers of old fashioned gardens. It is also possible to make gardens of native plants which have distinctively coloured foliage and to a lesser extent native gardens of plants which have contrasting foliage shapes and plant forms.

The increased selection of colourful natives and those with interesting variations from the usual foliage patterns and forms of growth, now available are not without their problems. Enthusiastic collectors of native plants, keenly aware of their intrinsic value and ever alert to the collectable value of subtle variations in flower, form and foliage were happy enough to provide within their gardens the microclimates and special conditions that plants gathered from a very broad geographic range need. In the case of Australia, for instance, 'native' plants range from those found in subtropical rainforest to those found in alpine meadows and semi-desert regions; some have patterns of growth based on summer rains, others are used to winter rains, while others still are adapted to growing only when unpredictable and infrequent desert thunderstorms bring rain. Collectors of native plants, be they Australian, South African or from California, may have sufficient interest in maintaining such diverse collections that they are prepared for the work involved to achieve a harmonious congregation of native plants in a 'bushland' garden

setting. This is highly skilled and specialised stuff, requiring experience and expertise
in seed harvesting, seed raising, tip pruning and tip propagation at the appropriate
stages of plant growth and according to seasonal variations; maybe making
specialised composts and creating specialised growing conditions. The likes of
Leschenaultia, Anigozanthos, Brachycome multifida, Clianthus formosa, Actinotus helianthii,

Scaevola, Telopea and *Dampiera* do produce stunning floral displays that can, in the hands
of an able gardener, create a ravishingly beautiful bush garden. Ordinary home
gardeners trying to achieve the same idyllic bushland setting, believing the plants to
be native and therefore hardy and requiring low maintenance are likely to face
disappointment. Natives are not necessarily easy.

1
6
3

PREVIOUS PAGES:

(p. 162) Kunzia
baxteri (top)
Grevillea
thelemanniana
(centre)
Sturt's desert
pea, Clianthus
formosus
(bottom)
(p. 163) Sheets
of ice plant,
Lampranthus
spectabilis
carpet the
ground at the
Karoo
Gardens,
Worcester,
South Africa.

Landscapers have also found in natives a ready source of low water-use plants that are suitable for covering large areas of ground, often in raw and exposed development sites and along transport corridors. Requiring minimal maintenance once the plants are established, the economics and 'political correctness' of such plantations are attractive to many urban planning authorities. Native plants selected for their ability to survive without additional water during the months of summer drought have also found a new use in domestic landscapes as designers have developed the concept of gardens having areas of high water need, low water need and minimal water need. Plants previously thought unattractive for garden use have suddenly found an acceptable role. An added bonus of some of these plants is their low flammability in bushfires; a careful selection of these planted in broad belts at the boundaries of properties can effectively reduce the potential for serious fire damage as well as save on water bills and create a unified landscape with other adjacent properties in areas where territorial limits are not marked by fences.

'Political correctness' seems to have taken hold of gardening with native plants too; at least in respect of the planting of urban parks and gardens, and in the planting of street trees. The ideas put about by proponents of these arguments for the exclusive use of native plants have been based on worthy ideas about saving biodiversity and recreating the 'natural' environment, regenerating bushland and restoring animal habitats. They also tend to be founded on personal visions and small-scale actions that do not necessarily take account of the reality that as communities we are where we are, and that we will continue to inhabit the places we presently inhabit. We cannot turn back the clock and pretend that migration and settlement of our respective countries never took place, and few of us would be able to live the supposedly eco-friendly lifestyles developed by the previous dominant cultures that ours have replaced. Nor has there been, until the advent of Tim Flannery's book *the future eaters* a comprehensive survey of the established scientific facts relating to these issues that sets in perspective the efficacy of the steps that have so far been taken to conserve the environment by providing the necessary thorough background information. With the information provided by Flannery, those whose views are polarised about the political correctness of purist gardens of native plants will have just as many of their preconceptions challenged as those who practice strict vegetable apartheid.

While there are plenty of enthusiasts for gardens where natives are grown exclusively, there is an even larger number of gardeners who are happily mixing plants native to Australia, South Africa, the Mediterranean basin, Chile and California as they seek to make their own gardens in the sun. Establishing a sense of place through the creation of personal landscapes and domestic environments will require more than an acknowledgment of the superficial issue of native *vs* exotic; it will need an exploration of the world of plants to discover those which can thrive where we live and an understanding of the necessary steps gardeners must take to ensure the wellbeing of native species — especially by taking responsibility to ensure that there are no weedy escapees from our gardens.

It is my belief that by a responsible exploration of the world for plants from climates similar to that in which we garden, a palette of plants equal to that of the cool climates of the gardening world will be developed. Our own efforts at seed raising and propagation are the first important steps. These can be supplemented by the advantages of modern techniques available to the horticultural industry once they are awakened to the growing appreciation and demand for such plants. Further afield, collecting across the habitat ranges of plants and hybridising will expand even further the scope for more closely matching plants with local conditions. The potential exists; it is slowly being realised; we will be able to give up old ways and old traditions that do nor serve our gardening well and use the developing 'new' garden flora of places where summers are warm and dry to create all kinds of our own gardens of the sun. Wherever we live, the future looks like an exciting mix of native plants and exotics. Would it be too much to suggest a kind of horticultural multiculturalism?

'A' IS FOR agapanthus

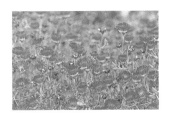

What's this? A chapter about agapanthus! 'Boring, boring, boring.' I hear you mutter while your thumb and forefinger itch to flick over the next few pages to skip the most obvious, and the most willing plant for gardens where the summer sun is hot and shines long. Can there be anything that is not known about agapanthus? There are two, either blue or white, are there not? They are evergreen and ever tough, no?

Yes, and every garden that ever was in sunny California, Australia, Spain, Greece, South Africa or the isles of the Mediterranean has hordes of them. True, true but there is more. Consider this list (the first and last of its kind in this book I trust; see how much more informative later entries are for the genera *Beschorneria*, *Xanthorrhoea*, *Yucca* and *Zamia*):

PREVIOUS PAGES:

(p. 166) Beth
Chatto is one
gardener who
has explored
the world of
plants to find
what is best
suited to her
gravel garden
at White Barn
House.
(p. 167)
Lampranthus
aurantiacus

Agapanthus africanus

Agapanthus campanulatus 'Albus'

Agapanthus campanulatus 'Isis'

Agapanthus campanulatus subsp. *campanulatus*
    'Hardingsdale'

Agapanthus campanulatus subsp. *patens*

Agapanthus caulescens subsp. *angustifolius*
    'Politique'

Agapanthus coddii

Agapanthus comptonii subsp. *comptonii*

Agapanthus dyerii

Agapanthus inapertus 'Inky Tears'

Agapanthus inapertus subsp. *hollandii*
    'Lydenburg'

Agapanthus inapertus subsp. *hollandii* 'Sky'

Agapanthus inapertus subsp. *inapertus* 'White'

Agapanthus inapertus subsp. *intermedius*
    'Wolkberg'

Agapanthus inapertus subsp. *pendulus* 'Graskop'

Agapanthus praecox 'Pallida'

Agapanthus praecox 'Plenus'

Agapanthus praecox subsp. *minimus* 'Adelaide'

Agapanthus praecox subsp. *minimus* 'Storms
    River'

Agapanthus praecox subsp. *orientalis*

Agapanthus praecox subsp. *orientalis* 'Mt
    Thomas'

Agapanthus walshii

Add to these:

Agapanthus x 'Ardernei'

Agapanthus x 'Ben Hope'

Agapanthus x 'Blue Baby'

Agapanthus x 'Blue Giant'

Agapanthus x 'Bressingham Blue'

Agapanthus x 'Buckingham Palace'

Agapanthus x 'Delft'

Agapanthus x 'Diana'

Agapanthus x 'Dutch Giant'

Agapanthus x 'Headbourne Hybrids'

Agapanthus x 'Lilliput'

Agapanthus x 'Loch Hope'

Agapanthus x 'Luly'

Agapanthus x 'Molly Fenwick'

Agapanthus x 'Olinda'

Agapanthus x 'Queen Anne'

Agapanthus x 'Rosemary'

Agapanthus x 'Swan Lake'

Agapanthus x 'Tom Thumb'

Agapanthus x 'Wavy Navy'

Plus at least three varieties with
variegated leaves

Agapanthus praecox subsp. *orientalis* 'Aureo-
    vittatus'

Agapanthus praecox subsp. *minimus* 'Variegatus'

Agapanthus x 'Jahan'

Agapanthus x 'Snoopy'

That makes well over forty different kinds. But there is not much information there on which to base a selection either according to habit, or colour or suitability to a warm, dry climate. A list is just a beginning for an adventurous garden maker. What can be found among the tribe of agapanthi? Some tall, some dwarf, some white, some ice blue, some richest cobalt, some inky blue-black, some massive, others graceful, some broad and strappy of leaf while others bear leaves that are narrow and grassy. Yes, they do come in white or blue, but such variations give rise to many possibilities in enriching

a garden. How the blues can sing of summer under a bright blue sky; how pure and
snowy the whites dazzling in strong sunlight. What luxury their deep green leaves,
prolific and vigorous even in times of drought. Only the so-called 'pink' agapanthus is of
dubious value; a curiosity in that the death throes of each half-shrivelled petal merely
turns them a shade of mawkish pink a few moments before they fall to earth. An
insufficient reason for planting it if ever one were proposed! All the rest are excellent
hardy plants worthy of a gardener's consideration.

Perhaps this will give you some ideas about the limited way we sometimes think
about 'common' plants; they are not always so common after all. A list such as I have
given above can be a useful guide to the discovery of plants new to our experience. But
what about discovering other 'new' plants? Learning how to think more widely about
what plants may suit our gardens is not so easy at first; the trick is to get out of the habit
of eschewing common plants and to get into the habit of finding out more about plants
that succeed in the climates where we live. We need to ask ourselves 'Are there any
other plants in this family or genus that might do well in this garden?'.

We need to do some research. 'Where will I get information about this family of
plants?'

We need to do some armchair shopping. 'Which nurseries and plant societies
might deal in plants like these?'

And then we need to try out plants to discover whether or not they will grow.

'B' IS FOR BESCHORNERIA

Beschorneria yuccoides is a most arresting plant with strappy silver foliage arranged in a large
rosette. Each somewhat succulent leaf is dotted sparsely with dull purplish spots. In
summer, mature rosettes send out a tall reddish pink spike that is eventually crowned with
a mass of large bright pink bracts from which vivid green tubular flowers hang down.

'C' IS FOR CEANOTHUS

Ceanothus is a genus of low shrubs and small trees from California. Most garden forms
have intensely blue flowers. There are prostrate forms well-suited as groundcovers such
as *Ceanothus gloriosus*, *C. griseus* and *C. maritimus*, and cultivars like 'Yankee Point', 'Hurricane
Point', 'Point Sierra'. Other California lilacs, as *Ceanothus* are commonly known, grow into
dense shrubs as in the case of 'Julia Phelps' and 'Joyce Coulter', while some will make
small shrubby trees large enough to garden under so long as the soil is not watered
heavily in summer. 'Blue Pacific' and 'Owlswood Blue' are two excellent selections of

taller-growing kinds. There are deciduous varieties too: 'Gloire de Versailles' and 'Henri de Fosse' are prominent among these, and more recently white forms like 'Snow Flurry', 'Snowball' and 'Popcorn' have been introduced to gardens. In general, ceanothus are not long-lived plants; about 10 to 15 years seems to be the lifetime of a plant before it begins to deteriorate, die back and collapse. This is not such a terrible fault; the plants are glorious while they are young and full of vigour, and their eventual decline offers the exciting prospect of finding a replacement, or the pleasure of growing the same plant again.

Without going through the entire alphabet — it would be tedious reading, and showing-off on my part — take what follows as examples of the scope for exploring the world of plants for exciting xerophytes.

X is for Xanthorrhoea

Xanthorrhoea quadrangulata is a short-stemmed/trunked variety of grasstree growing to 1 m; almost stemless are *Xanthorrhoea hastilis* and *X. bracteata* while *X. arborea*, among others, makes a trunk that may reach 3 to 4 m after many, many years. These plants are native to Australia, where they grow in open grasslands and sparse bushland; they are frequently found on very rough ground, rocky hillsides and are very hardy and drought-resistant. Seedlings are slow to establish but may be the only means of obtaining plants in countries outside Australia. Mature plants can be successfully transplanted though great care is needed to preserve as much of the rootball as possible. Most plants dug from the wild under licence from conservation authorities are given a period of recovery care to ensure that they are capable of re-establishing in gardens. Xanthorrhoeas have a singular appearance that stands out in any landscape; a thick black trunk topped with a dense mop of gently down-curving dull grey-green leaves may rise as much as three metres from the ground. At flowering time a tall, narrow black spear of tiny pale cream flowers may rise up above another two metres or so.

Yucca elata plants at Van Nuys, California.

1
7
0

Some species have the habit of twisting and looping the flower stem in a fascinating contortion that is much admired for its astonishing appearance. Flower arrangers who follow modern Japanese schools of design such as sogetsu and ikebana like to use such stems to add a touch of distinction to their art.

Y IS FOR YUCCA

Yuccas are a very distinguished group of plants from America with architectural qualities of boldness, stature and striking silhouette that at once marks them as ideal for creating that special exclamation mark or full stop that gives point or finality to a piece of gardening. As a rule they are very tolerant of hard conditions and all dislike wet, ill-draining soils. Some make very large plants, almost tree-like in their appearance, e.g., Joshua tree (*Yucca brevifolia*), soap tree (*Y. elata*), Spanish dagger (*Y. gloriosa*) and *Y. guatamalensis* (syn. *Y. elephantipes*). A few are virtually stemless, such as the well-known (*Yucca whipplei*), or 'Our-Lord's-Candle' so impressive are its towering multi-branched spires of creamy white bells. Some species have very stiff leaves with a single, strong end spine that require placement of the plants away from paths and patios. Some also have very hard,

sharp leaf edges which can easily cut fingers, arms and legs. Again, sensible placement away from places where people pass or gather will allow the refined beauty of the elegant flowers and distinguished foliage to be fully enjoyed.

Scan seedlists and nursery catalogues to discover plants that might find a place in some part of your garden making. Any of the following are worth further research and planning:

Yucca aloifolia, one of the taller clustering forms which may attain 3 m or more. The leaves are dark grey-green and held in stiff rosettes. The compact flower heads, solid with white blooms are shown well clear of the foliage.

Yucca baccata, blue yucca, clumps of several rosettes each with narrow erect leaves about 1 m high. The foliage is distinctly blue-grey and the short flower stems carry typical bell-shaped blooms that are purple brown on the outside.

Yucca brevifolia (syn. *Y. arborescens*) Perhaps the best known of the tree-like yuccas, the Joshua tree and a familiar sight to travellers in the deserts of Arizona, California, Utah and Nevada. The mature plants are magnificent and to be treasured and preserved; they do not transplant readily so smaller seed-raised specimens must be the choice of most gardeners wishing to grow it.

Yucca elata, a tall growing species that eventually attains tree-like proportions. Narrow grey foliage.

Yucca filamentosa 'Adam's needle', low growing rosettes of rather lax foliage with a few long wisps of white thread on the leaf margins. There are many variations on the theme.

Yucca filamentosa subsp. *concava*, very broad silver leaves tinged red in winter which make low, rather flattened rosettes from which develop fine spires of creamy white bells. It is among the most reliable in flowering every year once it is established.

Yucca filamentosa 'Brighteye' — yellow central stripe.

Yucca filamentosa 'Elegantissima' — by implication a somehow more refined selection.

Yucca filamentosa 'Garland's Gold' — vivid gold central stripes.

Yucca filamentosa 'Rosenglocke' — the flowers are pinkish on the outside.

Yucca filamentosa 'Schneefichte' (which translates as snow spruce).

Yucca filamentosa 'Variegata' — pale yellow stripes on the outside of each leaf.

Yucca flaccida 'Ivory' — very soft, pliable leaves that form a loose fountain of grey foliage variegated cream.

Yucca glauca, a species with very narrow grey leaves with conspicuous white threads of fibre attached to their edges. The plants form low rosettes and make short, unbranched spires hung with typical creamy white bells.

Yucca gloriosa 'Nobilis' (syn. *Y.* x 'Ellacombei', supposedly a superior cultivar). A strong-growing species with many selected varieties, of which this is but one. The deep green leaves are strong, long and stiff, thus giving rise to the common name 'Spanish dagger'. As they age the plants develop multi-trunked canopies of rosettes about 5 m high and slightly more across. Short spires of white bell-shaped flowers.

Yucca gloriosa 'Superba' — a form with silvery leaves and a short, dense flower spike.

Yucca gloriosa 'Variegata' — a cultivar in which the leaves are strikingly variegated with creamy white stripes.

Yucca guatamalensis (syn. *Y. elephantipes*), one of the tree forms that can grow 4 m tall and more with many trunks and branches, hence taking up a great deal of space and only for very large gardens — even if it does take fifty years or more to see it get going. Short spires of white bells.

Yucca recurvifolia — rosettes of rather soft and flexible leaves of blue-grey that eventually develop short stems about 2 m tall. Open spires of white flowers in spring.

Yucca recurvifolia 'Elegans Marginata' — soft yellow variegation on the leaf margins.

Yucca recurvifolia 'Variegata' — a soft yellow stripe down the centre of each leaf adds a touch of colour to the blue-green leaves.

Yucca whipplei subsp. *caespitosa* or *Y. whipplei.* subsp. *intermedia* are both good clump-forming varieties to about 3 m, sometimes the flowers are purplish stained on their outsides

Yucca 'Vittorio Emmanuele II' — an old European hybrid with creamy white flowers heavily stained with purple on the stems and on the outside of each petal. It is thought to be a hybrid of *Y. aloifolia* and so can be expected to develop a shrubby habit as it matures.

Z IS FOR ZAMIA

Zamia furfuracea is a cycad from Mexico with tough foliage that resembles a prehistoric fern — which it almost is. It makes a grand tub plant in areas where frosts may damage its leaves and can be grown under the shelter of trees. There are many other cycads too. Most are not easy to get and are very slow-growing so large-sized plants can be very expensive, but a few seedlings can make an attractive and exotic potted collection. Look out also for varieties of *Cycas*, *Dioon* and *Encephalartos*.

There is also the perennial *Zauschneria californica* (California fuchsia — syn. *Epilobium californica*) and the *Zephyranthes* (rain lily) which comes in approximately thirty-five species.

The range is huge. The chase is exciting. The rewards are hardy plants and beautiful gardens for warm, dry climates.

1

7

3

manavlins

For Mavens

manav(i)lins: *I dare say a word or two of explanation is warranted here. I came upon this unusual word quite by accident when thumbing through a set of Euan Cox's* The New Flora and Sylva (1928–1940), *which I had bought from Dan Lloyd one year at Chelsea. The word 'manavlins' stood out in one of the article headings.*

Looking back through the volume I found there was a series of articles by Clarence Elliott, a well-known plant collector of the day. It was, he explained, a very useful though archaic word, and not much used. According to the *Shorter Oxford Dictionary* its meaning is 'odds and ends'. And that is why it came to be here, for this chapter is about odds and ends of the plant world that might be worth chasing up for trial in gardens of the kind we are thinking about in this book.

PREVIOUS PAGES:

(p. 174) The

gardens of

Tresco Abbey

in the Scilly

Isles provide a

fine setting for

many plants

such as Echium

fastuosum

which is

considered

tender in the

rest of

England.

(p. 175)

Artemisia x

'Powis Castle',

Ascot

And what of **mavens**? Another word I have collected; this time from that particular set of young, American gardening writers who have, so it seems, been to writers' graduate school and come away with suitably improved wordpower and a repertoire of esoteric words with which to amuse themselves and puzzle their readers. I once determined to record all such words I came across in my reading, but gave up when most of them failed to appear in the pages of my dictionary. As you can see my dictionary is not such a small one, but dashing off to the public library to consult the voluminous *Oxford Dictionary* was more than I could be bothered with when there were better things to do in the garden.

MAVENS (*US slang, Yiddish*) Expert or connoisseur

Now let us consider *Manavlins for Mavens.*

Since I sat down to write this book four years have passed, a longer time than I had planned, but that can't be helped, and the passage of time allows me the luxury of changing my mind about a few things. One thing I have changed my mind about, though not completely, is the usefulness of lists. Now there are lists and lists; some endlessly dull, some informative and some useful for catalysing action. There are lists with entries so brief they are almost useless and there are lists so complicated with abbreviations they take a month to decipher. There are lists that repeat old information and describe the commonplace and there are those that bring to attention new things and stimulate fresh perspectives. Plant lists can be among the most awful, especially those constructed to the dictate of some publisher's design team where fashion considerations all too often overrule pragmatism and practical design. There can also be plant lists written in books that stimulate new gardening ideas and plant associations and I trust you will indulge me if I break my own rule about not making lists, to bring my readers a selection of interesting experimental plants for warm, dry climates.

Asarina antirrhinifolia — a small, lightweight climber from the south-western states of the United States where it is sometimes known as the snapdragon vine. The plant is winter deciduous and cold-tolerant. The antirrhinum-like flowers may be purple, pink or red and are borne throughout the warm months, especially if a little water is given from time to time. The vine will scramble 3 m or so given support.

Azara microphylla — a small tree from Chile with tiny, dark green, glossy leaves and upright somewhat sparse growth to 4 m or so. In late winter yellow flowers, so tiny they are hardly noticed, appear in the leaf axils on the undersides of the leaves. The vanilla-chocolate scent is wonderful in the late afternoon and early evening.

Baccharus pilularis 'Twin Peaks' — a selected form of the coyote bush from San Francisco County in California. Prostrate growth, very small evergreen foliage, insignificant flowers but needs some summer moisture. A tougher variety is found in *Baccharis* x 'Centennial' which can withstand higher temperatures and much drier conditions. This plant is frost-tolerant and is always a rich green mat of leaves and small twiggy growths. It can be trimmed to maintain a very compact form, otherwise it will slowly mound up to around 1 m high.

Bomarea kalbreyeri — one of the so-called climbing alstromerias and not all that tolerant of drought, but it has such spectacular flowers and needs warm, frost-free conditions to perform well that it could be considered as a likely candidate for that special spot in a part of the garden that gets watered through summer. Twining stems of evergreen foliage support hanging bunches of large tubular orange-red and yellow flowers spotted with dark red. There are other species too that would be worth the trouble of raising from seed. The plants are native to Mexico and areas south-west in Brazil, Peru and Chile.

Buddleia auriculata — a winter-flowering butterfly bush with silvered foliage and very fragrant creamy white flowers. Shrubby at first, but grows taller; can benefit from hard pruning to invigorate strong flowering growth. Many buddleias new to cultivation are being introduced. They need to be tried in warm, dry gardens. *Buddleia marrubiifolia* from Texas and northern Mexico is a proven dry climate species with small 'bobbles' of burnt orange flowers and should be more widely planted. Like all buddleias, its soft growth is frost tender.

Buddleia CLD 1377 — is from a collection made in China by an expedition of the Edinburgh Botanic Gardens. It is summer flowering and produces well-scented lilac flowers with a small yellow throat. It is hard to say how drought-tolerant it may be; who is willing to try such things to the death? Not me. There are many others from this expedition being raised from seed and introduced on a trial basis. No doubt the good performers will be sorted out from the duds as the next few years show up their assets and faults.

Buddleia pichinchensis — a newly introduced species from Ecuador that deserves a wide trial. The rounded clusters of bright yellow flowers that turn dark orange as they develop are displayed against snowy silver-felted foliage. Ken Gillanders, who introduced this species, made no note at the time of any perfume; most likely he was already busily looking ahead to see what new treasure lay just ahead.

Canna x 'Durban' — a vividly tropical-looking plant with deep purple-red leaves boldly marked with pink veins. Admittedly not really drought-tolerant, it would be a striking accent to some favourable sunny corner or as a pot plant that sparks 'Wow!' from everyone who sees it. It is renamed 'Tropicana' in Australia.

Capparis spinosa — the genuine caper plant from the Mediterranean whose pickled flower buds (not the fruits) we enjoy with meats and fish. The plant is prostrate, prickly and ornery. Just try to grow one. One speck of kindness or attention and it expires in a pique. Leave it strictly alone in a hard, stony ground and it may surprise you by growing. Should you be so fortunate it may develop surprising pink and white flowers, and eventually fruits. I had one once but ... Well, you all know that story; it's an inevitable part of trying to grow new plants, even when they do come from places similar to your own stamping ground. I must try it again some day soon.

Carissa macrocarpa — the Natal plum with spreading evergreen grown, rich dark green foliage that is tough, tough, tough and concealing below each leaf joint a pair of vicious spines. Delightfully perfumed starry white flowers belie the armature of this plant.

Euphorbia cooperii is an astonishing succulent 'tree'.

As a hedge and high ground cover it is excellent. Tolerant of salty winds and harsh conditions. *Carissa bispinosa* is a similar species which is somewhat taller.

Clematis viorna — a delightful and tough low climber to about 3 m. Wiry growth and small leaves with small vase-shaped flowers of violet, pinkish or purplish hues in midsummer. The flowers have thick, leathery petals and no discernible perfume. Similar and curiously interesting species are *Clematis crispa*, *Clematis texensis* and *Clematis versicolor*.

All come from various parts of the United States and seem fairly hardy because of their stout, far-reaching root systems. Another delightful small-flowered species is *Clematis campaniflora* from Portugal. It produces masses of pale blue bells with strongly recurved petals in midsummer; it grows about 3 m high given something to latch onto and is very easy from seed. For a scented clematis that is drought-tolerant look for *Clematis flammula* from Europe. It is easy from seed, perhaps too easy if you are as successful as I have been with it. The best sources of seed seem to be the various European and American rock garden and alpine society seed lists.

Crocus species — a genus of about 80 species of small bulbs with almost as many subspecies and many more forms and selected cultivars. Many come from around the Mediterranean basin and eastward into Turkey and central Asia. The greatest number come from Turkey and are very well adapted to a regimen of winter rainfall and summer drought. Just the sort of plants we are looking for. Without doubt the best sources are the seed lists of alpine and rock garden societies. Some species seem a bit miffy about competing in the hurly-burly of rough grass and among the moss and roots at the bases of deciduous trees, but there are many that are at home almost anywhere. Kinds like *Crocus tomasinianus, Crocus nudiflorus, Crocus hadriaticus, Crocus veluchensis, Crocus pulchellus* and

The tall bulbs and stiff, dark green foliage of Crinum asiaticum *show off the large heads of sweetly perfumed white flowers.*

1
7
9

Crocus speciosus will self-sow with a willingness in garden beds, in gravel pathways, in rough grass that is mown now and then — almost everywhere but places that are deeply shaded and wet underfoot. Search them out; they are easy from seed and will flower within a few years of being raised.

Cyclamen species — all but a few of the little wild cyclamen are desirable and attractive bulbs that are well-adapted to gardens in warm, dry areas. Grown under shrubs and trees they will prosper and multiply well with minimal care, apart from weeding out other plants which might smother them and keeping a check on snails and slugs. Bulbs are easily raised from seed; the autumn and winter growing species are probably easiest to start with; look for *Cyclamen coum, Cyclamen purpurescens, Cyclamen hederifolium, Cyclamen cilicium, Cyclamen balearicum, Cyclamen creticum, Cyclamen graecum, Cyclamen libanoticum, Cyclamen cyprium* and *Cyclamen persicum*. These should be trouble free in most Mediterranean-type climates; as you can see from the Latinised specific names they come from around the shores of the Mediterranean Sea. There are dozens of forms and varieties with distinctive leaf patterns and flower colours; all lovely and well worth growing. Depending on where your garden is, you could even expect to grow the reputedly difficult north African *Cyclamen rohlfsianum* outdoors. At least it has that reputation among enthusiasts in cooler, wetter climates. See how you go.

Dahlia imperialis 'Alba' — a white-flowered variant of the more usual lilac pink giant tree dahlia. Newly introduced from seed collected by Dr Keith Hammett of Auckland, the plants are just now sufficiently well established for propagating material to be harvested. There are two forms getting about; one is a single-flowered kind while the other has an anemone centre. Both flower in autumn after making strong growth all summer, provided a soaking is given every month or so. The stems resemble those of a stout bamboo and reach 3 m and more under good conditions. Plants can be grown from internodal stem cuttings struck in coarse sand from early summer onwards.

Eriogonum giganteum — St Catherine's lace. How did this plant escape attention for so long? It is one of the better kept horticultural secrets of California. It is adaptable to soils and sites, very drought-tolerant and able to be pruned into interesting mature forms. It has white flowers and silver foliage, and more — its flowers dry well for indoor use. There are dozens of other species too, including many dry alpine forms which need to be 'discovered' by gardeners.

Euphorbia broteri — a comparative newcomer to gardens is this spurge from Spain; apparently a close relative of *Euphorbia rigida*, this species has reddish orange flower bracts whereas the latter has them coloured the usual acid green. Both have stiff but trailing stems clad with lance-shaped silver leaves and a spread of 75 cm or so. Jan Waddington, who specialises in euphorbias at her nursery at Kergunyah in Victoria says that *Euphorbia broteri* has a more open habit; my plant has yet to develop that characteristic, and as we all learn from each other I'm content to pass along her observation.

Euphorbia cyparissias — a willing doer and very hardy in dry conditions. My plants came from Dame Elisabeth Murdoch and I'm very grateful for the gift. The plant is native to much of Europe and has, for that reason, been regarded by many discriminating gardening authorities as rather too commonplace for planting in gardens. Those who do not garden in Europe will quickly appreciate what an excellent plant it is for difficult, dry positions. It spreads by suckers and makes a low mound of fine-leaved silvery foliage that bears small heads of greeny-yellowy flowers. It colonises well and makes good ground cover in parts of my garden where no water is used during summer. The drought helps to curb its willingness to increase without sapping its growth. I like it mixed with the dwarf forms of *Vinca minor.*

Euphorbia nicaeensis — a compact rather sprawling sub-shrub with an appearance that is somewhat similar to *Euphorbia myrsinites*. That sounds rather off-putting doesn't it? It is a fine garden plant with potential along the edges of low, drystone walls where it's habits of growth can be shown off. Yes, it has similarities with the more strongly prostrate *Euphorbia myrsinites*, but is quite distinctly more upright. The euphorbias are a tribe yet to be fully appreciated for their value in warm, dry gardens. Lawrence Johnston had a whole garden of them at Hidcote when he gardened there, but these were lost after he retired to live in France. The potential is there and should be explored. Look for species from the Mediterranean basin, Turkey and central Asia; the sub-alpine forms from the Himalayas and Asia are less drought tolerant, indeed some require plenty of summer moisture. Some fine selected clones are beginning to appear. Particularly useful in warm, dry gardens are *Euphorbia characias* subsp. *'wulfenii'* in its forms 'John Tomlinson' and 'Lambrook Gold'; the variegated forms are too susceptible to sun scorch and dryness at the roots to be useful in our gardens.

Heptacodium miconidides (syn. *Heptacodium jasminoides*) — a hardly known recent introduction from China which is reported to flower well where summers are warm. It is a shrubby plant with leaves resembling those of a lilac and is a member of the honeysuckle family. The scented white flowers appear in late summer in large heads and they come close to looking like orange blossom. It is also said to colour well in autumn, but who knows how it may perform in warm, dry climates? China is a big place with a very varied flora; it sounds as if *Heptacodium miconidides* may be worth looking into.

1
8
1

Lathyrus chloracanthus — a yellow-flowered member of the sweet pea family and probably a perennial in warm, dry climates. Not a plant for bone dry parts of the garden but delightful in those places adjacent to outdoor living areas where some water is given. 3 m.

Montanoa bipinnatifida — a strange giant tree daisy from Mexico which is sometimes found in old gardens. The plants grow about 3 m tall and are composed of towering stems bearing opposite pairs of large, deeply toothed and cut leaves. As summer turns into autumn terminal heads of white daisies are produced in profusion. The nearest simile I can call to mind would be an all-white form of the garden annual cineraria (*Senecio cruentus* hybrids). The plant is statuesque, intriguing and handsome but does need a frost-free climate.

Opuntia basilaris — the beavertail prickly pear that is native to Utah, Nevada, California, Arizona, Baja California and Sonora, Mexico. A very attractively coloured cactus with round blue-grey leaf pads dotted with small clusters of tiny spines (glochids rather than thorns) and silken-textured flowers of bright magenta pink closely packed along the rims of the pads. The dry fruits do not develop attractive succulent 'pears', or *tunas* as other species do. A stately accent plant that will grow to about 2 m high and somewhat wider. Plants are easily raised by rooting entire leaf pads set in sand once the severing cut has callused.

Puya chiliensis, Huntington Botanic Gardens, San Marino, California

Opuntia engelmannii — another prickly pear; this one also from the south-western United States. It has very large, rounded, pale-green pads regularly set with small clusters of long, grey spines. Bright yellow flowers are carried in large numbers along the margins of each leaf pad and as these ripen their seed pods the fruits swell into

succulent, dark red *tunas* which are edible and decorative. Mature plants form mounds of branching growth about 1.5 m high and 3 m wide.

    Opuntia santa-rita — the Santa-Rita prickly pear. This plant has very distinctively coloured, round leaf pads of silver blue with deeper purple tints along the leaf edges. This coloration is more strongly marked during drought or cold weather. The yellow flowers appear in spring and over summer the seed pods ripen as fat, juicy oval *tunas* that are coloured purple. Like all opuntias, this prickly pear has its share of spines and glochids.

The Desert Garden of the Huntington Botanic Gardens is the place to get close to Puya coerulea *(above).* Puya chiliensis *(left).*

1
8
3

Paliuris spina-christi — Christ's thorn. A plant curio from a wide range of countries spreading across southern Europe to northern China. The shrubby growth reaches about 2 m in height and produces flowers of no great significance that result in fruits that look like miniature coolies' hats about 3 cm across. The plant bears twin thorns at the base of each leaf and for this reason should be planted away from paths and patios. This drawback notwithstanding, it is an interesting and adaptable plant.

Pancratium maritimum — also known commonly in Europe as the sea daffodil. This fine bulb grows in the sand drifts away from the water's edge but very close to the shoreline around the western Mediterranean. Seriously over-collected and now depleted in the wild, but readily raised from seed and a wonderful reward for the patient gardener. The plants flower 'naked' at the end of summer; the flowers are white and wonderfully scented. To perform well, the bulbs must be baked in summer, though a light covering of dried leaves and grass would prevent the bulbs cooking. *Pancratium illyricum* from Crete and Sardinia is similar, but evergreen. Fabled and fabulous.

Pistacia lentiscus — the lentisc or mastic shrub of the Mediterranean region. Evergreen, fine pinnate foliage with four pairs of leaflets and one terminal leaflet and densely packed clusters of tiny flowers that ripen small, black, edible fruits. The plants take trimming well and could stand as a fair replacement for box in warm, dry areas. Mature plants can be limbed up to make small trees with wonderful gnarled old trunks and branches.

Punica granatum — the well-known pomegranate. Less well-known are the double, white-flowered form *Punica granatum* 'Alba Plena' and *Punica granatum* 'Mme Legrelle' which produces double red flowers with a boldly marked white edge. All varieties make excellent large shrubs or, if limbed up, small spreading trees to 5 m if they are in a frost-free area. The shade they cast is dense and the trees are briefly deciduous. The foliage and stems seem not to be liked by grazing animals so where goats, sheep, horses and cows reach over the garden wall this plant has an added attraction.

Puya coerulea — a member of the bromeliad family from Chile with astonishing deep navy-blue, bell-shaped flowers massed on a stalk about 2 m high. The flowers have a distinctive metallic sheen and are eagerly worked by hummingbirds and other honeyeaters. The spiny rosettes of foliage mound up into growths of multiple heads and the flowers appear in late spring. The plants are drought-tolerant but dislike heavy frosts.

Equally stunning and even taller are *Puya alpestris* from Argentina and Chile with metallic teal blue-green flowers and *Puya chilensis* which has vivid chartreuse flowers just bronzed with khaki.

To see them at their best, go to the Huntington Botanic Gardens at San Marino in California in late April. Simply breathtaking.

Quercus phillyreoides — a handsome Japanese oak with rather shrubby growth and smallish, neat evergreen leaves that are downy beneath. It is not much grown but deserves wider planting for its ability to be trimmed up into a neat small tree. Mature trees can reach about 8 m in good conditions. The family of oaks is waiting to be tried more widely to see what they can do for our gardens. Outside England and the United States, where are the arboreta and trial grounds for the numerous species from mild climates?

Quercus rysophylla — an oak tree from Mexico with incredibly handsome leaves, glossy dark green, deeply veined and resembling those of a loquat tree with a tad more toothing along the edges. It looks as if it may be evergreen, and it looks as though it could be worth trying. Getting fresh, viable seeds could be the hardest part.

Salvia corrugata — yet another try-and-see new species from Ecuador. It sounds pretty interesting: 'an evergreen shrub to 3 m with 8 cm clusters of ultramarine blue flowers over a long period. Its attractive deeply rugose leaves are felted on the reverse side.' So says Ken Gillanders of a plant he collected and introduced. The world of salvias is large and still being explored by many admirers of the genus. To know them all intimately would be a lifetime's study and I don't have the inclination for that, though by our good fortune there are a hardy crowd who do, and the most I can do is state my admiration for the genus and point to a few that I find especially good. By all means follow up all possible sources. I am very partial to *Salvia gesneriflora*, a very tall-growing species with bold scarlet flowers and black calyxes set off by bright green leaves. In Kleine Lettunich's garden near Watsonville, California, where I collected some seed, the mature plants grew 4 m tall on the frost-free hillside. A knock-out plant if ever there was one! *Salvia buchananii* is exciting considerable interest among aficionados and I am keen to try *Salvia guaranitica* 'Argentine Skies' which is sky blue where the species is dark blue. Sue Templeton is leading the charge in Australia and I know she has found good support from keen collectors in the United States with whom she has made contact and established friendships — as must we all who would usefully add to the range of plants we grow.

Tagetes lemmoni — Mexican tree marigold, a soft-wooded shrub which in frost-free areas can eventually grow 2 m tall. The foliage is pungently scented with a very strong 'marigold' odour that some find overwhelming and oppressive. If you find, as I do, that it is a spicy scent it is more than acceptable in a corner of the garden where hot colours

1
8
5

are wanted. Throughout the warm months, small burnt-orange marigolds are spangled over the ferny leaves. It can be a bit floppy so the support of nearby plants can be a help. It seems homey enough for inclusion in a vegetable garden of the decorative kind.

Tulipa sylvestris — one of the obliging wild tulips; this species from Spain and Italy has delightful clear yellow flowers that open from sharply pointed green-tinted buds in the winter. It multiplies prodigiously from 'droppers' — small bulbils that form on long stolons as the 'mother' bulb is growing. It colonises under deciduous trees and in more open spaces and seems well equipped to deal with wet winters and dry summers. I find it has no diseases or pests, apart from slugs and snails. Try also the brassy orange *Tulipa orphanidea* from the mountains of Greece, *Tulipa biflora* which bears two white, starry flowers, the pink *Tulipa saxatilis* from Crete and the bold red *Tulipa agenensis* (syn. *Tulipa oculis-solis*) from the fields of southern Europe. I find the Lady tulip (*Tulipa clusiana*) rather more difficult as it seems to produce far more leaves that flowers and tends towards having off seasons every second year. It has flowers striped broadly with red and white on the outside and is worth every effort to get established. I must keep trying.

Urginea maritima — a common enough bulb of the curious kind, the sea squill hails from the sandy shores of the Mediterranean. It produces no flowers of distinction, though the 1.25 m stems are tall enough and each carries a hundred or so small whitish starry blooms; what is astonishingly good is the rosette of leaves that appear during

The sage family is noted for plants which are hardy and lovely, such as the hummingbird sage, Salvia spathacea *from California.*

winter and die off in summer. Each rosette is flattened and composed of twenty or so wavy-edged leaves; a large plantation of them looks rather good. Especially well suited for planting in quiet corners where truly tough ground cover is needed. These bulbs would look impressive planted along with broad swathes of other large bulbs with distinctive foliage such as *Haemanthus coccineus, Amaryllis belladonna* and any of the crinums.

Veltheimia capenis — a South African bulb that produces its foliage and flowers during the cooler, wetter months. The large clusters of tubular flowers are fairly well known, being carried on tall stalks

ABOVE: *Woolly blue curls,* Trichostema lanata, *relative of the salvias from California* **LEFT:** Salvia regia *cv 'Indigo Spires'*

and of a pleasing shade of rosy pink, but it is the foliage that is especially attractive. Each broad, glossy, bright apple-green leaf is distinctively waved along its edges and carried in a spreading rosette at ground level. A large grouping is very decorative while in leaf. The bulbs are succulent and tough, and easily propagated by removing the 'chips' that grow around the sides of each mature bulb. The leaves can suffer badly from hail damage and frost, thus spoiling the display — though flowers are usually still produced as the weather warms. There is a desirable cream-flowered form too, but it does seem more prone to cold damage, poor drainage and rotting off in cold weather.

Wigandia caracasana — a shrubby plant from the central American states which in lush conditions is sometimes reported as a climber. However, in drier climates it generally stays at about 1.5 m, spreading sideways to a considerable girth by suckering and layers. The plants produce large, fiddle-shaped leaves that are somewhat hairy and the stems are covered with irritating hairs. Treated with caution and planted away from outdoor living areas where it could come in contact with uncovered skin, its large heads of rich blue forget-me-not flowers can be enjoyed throughout summer. It is intolerant of frost and grows tolerably well with occasional watering during droughts. The dead flower stems are persistent so regular dead-heading will keep the plants tidy and encourage a succession of flowers.

Worsleya rayneri (syn. *Worsleya procera*) — most keen gardeners enjoy a challenge and here is one: the blue amaryllis from the cliff faces of the Organ Mountains of Brazil. It is a large bulb, about 1 m tall, topped with a dozen or so strong, rather stiff recurving leaves. It demands excellent drainage and is intolerant of frost. Don Barrett, who lives near me grows his bulbs in upturned terracotta drainage pipes filled mostly with gravel, pine bark, rice hulls and leaf mould. He feeds them frequently and keeps them always in full sun. It is reputed to take ten years and more to flower from seeds. He's still waiting. Bulbs recently offered for sale in England were priced at UK£95; at those prices it seems the wait is probably worth it! The large lily flowers, usually about six to eight on one stalk, are pale blue with darker edges. No-one records whether or not it is perfumed. Would that expectation be gilding the lily?

My critics will notice at least two — there may be more — things that I have missed out in this highly idiosyncratic selection of plants. The most glaring omission is the number of plants they like better than those above; plants that are more rare, more difficult, more beautiful. Mavens are sometimes like that, or so I'm told. The collecting bug sometimes bites them hard. Eagerly buying up one of everything (two if the plant is labelled 'rare') is a phase every keen gardener goes through; most of us come out the other side more discerning and more willing to experiment. A sad few get stung with the I've-got-something-you-haven't-got bug and stay all their lives in its clutches.

It will also be observed that there are few hybrids and named forms here. My reason is simply that I firmly believe the best hybrids for our own conditions are those raised and selected in our own particular conditions. Plants imported from other climatic areas have been bred, raised and selected according to their viability, vigour and flowering ability it conditions quite different to those that have a bearing on the success of plants in our own gardens. Can we wonder then, or complain if such 'alien' plants fail to do well? Try some imports by all means, especially if they originate in a climates similar to that where you live, but also try raising a few of your own hybrids. Pollinating flowers and raising seedlings to flowering can be absorbing, fun and sometimes profitable. Even if only seeds pollinated by the bees are raised there may well be some interesting results. Whether or not the plants that result are worth the bother of naming and officially registering with the appropriate authorities is another question altogther; the main consideration should be that they give pleasure and perform well.

One final point: always try unknown plants from places other than your own where the climate is warm and dry in summer and cool and wet in winter. It is easy enough to grow whatever is familiar through local gardens and nurseries. It can also be fatally boring for the development of a garden and for the making of a gardener. Live dangerously, buy a packet of seed.

THE TIME TO PLANT
crocuses

Making big changes in our gardens and making changes in the ways we think about gardening are sometimes difficult. Whether it is a big tree that has to go or new drains that have to be installed we come to accept the need for disruption and mess and raw earth very slowly. Our comfort zone is threatened and we passively resist making any decision that will change forever those things which help us feel settled and secure.

Conservatism lurks within the hearts of all. As gardeners we do not want to leave old gardens behind when we must move to new homes; it is not just the plants we would miss, but the routine and familiarity of tending them. Our intuition about dealing with soil, water, pests and weather is put at risk by unknown situations. Why would we then decide to change the way we garden?

Early in my experience as a garden consultant I was taken to see a garden made in the 1920s by a very prominent mercantile family. The house was a noted Art Deco structure with all the atmosphere of a ship; it was moored in a garden by a series of terraces and promenades; it was sunny and relaxed with strong, elegant lines and a presence that was truly majestic. Modern, purposeful — taking into its core the motor car, swimming pool, cocktails at five and long country house weekends. Yet its very power stifled any further development beyond the day it was completed. Sixty years and more had passed; trees and shrubs had grown, filling beds and blurring the design; plants had died leaving graceless gaps that revealed things best left unseen; gardeners toiled daily but produced nothing more than a kind of sullen, bald neatness. The present owner, whom I shortly met, was anxious for ideas about giving the garden a lift — he'd lived there all his life and he sensed something needed to be done to make the garden livelier and more interesting. He bustled out armed with a notebook and a charming manner; he showed me round from beginning to end; here steering me gently with a tap to my elbow, now waving me to inspect this bush like a policeman conducting road traffic, next nodding and smiling me to look over there. We discussed ideas continuously for three hours but all my suggestions crashed against the same sea wall. 'My Mother planted that …, planned that …, chose that …, loved that … and I couldn't change it.' Dashed by history on rocks of such strong sentiment and pounded by wave upon wave of heavy memories, my ideas were reduced to froth. I went away curious at being so lightly disregarded. Did this man want ideas or not? Perhaps he thought he had invented a new way to pass the time of day pleasantly? The garden was not so famous as the name of she who made it but that fame endured so long as her name was told, and the telling of it ensured the life and fame of her creation.

I returned almost ten years later. The garden had scarcely changed, though it had become even more overgrown, more trees had fallen, more limbs had dropped. More than ever, Mother ruled from the other side with an unheard siren song. The gardeners had changed — the old ones had probably died of boredom, and the new ones were struggling to cope with demands for improvement without radical removals, replacement without disruption and rejuvenation *sans* change. By now decrepitude was set in hard, but still things needful of doing were undone. Flaws seen but unseen were ignored; paths blocked by bulbous conifers, paving lifted akimbo by thick tree roots, terraces bursting and crumbling under the dead weight of plants and the plants themselves grown woody and flowerless to the point of senility. And still no changes were ordered. Seeing this I quickly developed a new perspective; for some change is just plain hard to achieve. The need for change is difficult to accept; the results of change are disturbed memories and discomforted sensibilities; the creating of change is tumultuous, tiring and threatening. Some just cannot bring themselves to it. The best course of action would be for me to go away quietly, without comment, but for some murmured thanks for the invitation and leave my host to his garden of memories.

How could it be, I wonder, that someone so successful in business lacked the confidence to take a pruning saw in hand and make some changes in his garden? Let us leave this poor soul trapped in the past and take a look at those caught perpetually in the future by their want of confidence.

As I write this it is the first day of spring. The serious national newspapers have columns devoted to serious gardening and at this important turn of the seasons their writers seriously ponder the garden fashions that will dominate the coming year. Some even survey ever so briefly the entire history of garden making in this country, but all focus strongly on what style, what plants and what books will lead the trends. Fashion victims readily rush out crying out 'Mondo, Mondo, Mondo' or some other horticultural catchcry that may, or may not answer their want of confidence in trusting their own ability to discern what will look good and do best in their own garden. Who cares anyway? If it doesn't work, fails to grow, dies or looks ratty there are always new ideas and plants to be sold and bought. A bevy of overseas experts will be imported to inspire new fashions, fresh plants will be introduced as answering all the failures of previous years, new gardens will be imposed on the bones of old disasters. The whole chain of events becomes a self-fulfilling cycle of delirium, dismay, dissatisfaction and desperate hope — and yet it continues to prop up a large part of the horticultural industry.

So what do the good taste gurus hold out to the fashion conscious gardener for the coming year this wet, wintry day? Can you guess? Of course, Mediterranean gardens are about to enjoy a vogue. Having disposed of English flower gardens, cottage gardens, historic recreations, period pieces, French gardens, Italian gardens and all the rest that went before, what else could it be? And what will come next, as it surely must? Those who haven't the confidence to follow their own instincts or who haven't the time to develop them will soon fall victim to some other dazzling idea imported from foreign parts this year for those condemned by uncertainty to be perpetual consumers. But when the *ennui* of silver-grey plants, spiky things, lavenders, rosemaries, olive and citrus trees, rock roses and pencil-slim cypresses is supplanted with the excitement of Tex-Mex or some other flamboyant flim-flam, will anything remain? Is there garden life and horticultural style after Provencal blue wrought-iron furniture, walls rusticated with

Rose's Terracotta Lime-Wash, and *vases d'Anduze, amphorae* and *pithoi*? I hope so. And I believe so.

Whatever comes next for the fashion-conscious, there will stay with some readers, many I hope, a few of the ideas that have been written about here that they have found fit comfortably with their own circumstances. It was not my intent to satisfy those who wish to establish themselves as trend leaders — this book would have been finished two years ago if that were so. I want to give some encouragement to those who want to make their garden a pleasant environment that suits their lifestyle and is at home with the climate, soil and circumstances. Whether it be the choice of plants, or ideas about design and features, or even just a tad of inspiration, it has been my wish to offer support and to suggest the possibilities of using our own situations as a springboard to developing fresh ideas and to creating a new gardening cosmognosis. A start has been made by many of those who contributed their experiences to my groundwork for this book; let us take a look at one in particular . . .

There are those who garden apart from the world of fanciful design and *faux* style, who garden according to the genius of their place, and who experiment and explore with plants to find what will grow and look good, and to find effective ways of putting them together to make gardens that are lovely to look at and satisfying to live with. On a windswept grassy hillside at La Honda just outside the conurbation of San Francisco, Betsy Clebsch has made her garden; a garden that excites all who are invited to see it; a garden that is gladsome to see and enthralling to its maker. Away from the house a rough palisade encloses a level part of a hillside; the enclosed space is backed by a glade of oaks on one side and on the other the steep fall of the land downhill creates a distant horizon of hills and a vast sky. Within the deer-proof fence the garden at first seems unremarkable, but for a few large boulders submerged like hippos in the growth. The design is apparent from the first glance. Simple paths wind through the beds of low shrubs and perennials, the spaces they enclose dictated largely by the too-hard-to-remove boulders and the maker's desire to encourage lingering and close inspection, and to indulge the toing and froing habits of plant lovers as they meander from one treasure that catches their eye to the next. There are no built structures or formality to impose on the splendour of the scenery. The garden is just there; a made thing but an unobtrusive foreground to the big sky. As I have said it all *seems* simple enough. But when you stop to look more closely, the garden reveals a diversity and richness of plants that is at once harmonious with the wider landscape of the hillside and also within itself. Sensitivity to the site has not dulled the urge to collect, but

1
9
4

GARDENS OF THE SUN

instead has served to focus the gardener's wit on discovering which plants will thrive and associate well together. Now this in itself is not so remarkable; despite what the glossies tell us *ad nauseam* there are thousands of knowing gardeners who are not constrained by the hunger for whatever-comes-next. Betsy Clebsch is clearly one such gardener. But her genius is not daring to be different. It lies in an altogether different direction. Her garden sits well in its landscape and she plainly takes great delight from working in it and in showing it to others. And it is when you are shown the garden that its *genius loci* is revealed. The plants are recognisable but are not commonly known; they are rare in cultivation, but not regarded as rarities by the gardener. There is none of that nasty possessiveness here that is found among some who love to have what others cannot have. Here the plants serve a purpose and that purpose is explained with enthusiasm and charm. Their purpose, apart from bringing beauty to the garden, is that they thrive in the warm, dry climate without intensive care. What is most remarkable is that most of the plants (or seeds of them) have been collected in the wild and come from areas with climates similar to that at La Honda. Betsy Clebsch has gone out in the wilderness to discover and collect plants for her garden. No quick trips to the local nurseries for her; no thumbing through mail-order catalogues searching for novelties and rarities. No easily scrawled cheques and convenient parcels in the post. Instead, the hard slog of hiking through rough, lonely places and travelling among the people of other cultures to explore for plants that will suit her garden and enrich the making of it with memories and new possibilities. The getting of them has grown out of a determination to have a garden of plants that need no cosseting to flourish; the garden made with them has grown out of a desire to garden in harmony with her environment, and the sharing of knowledge and plants has come about because of Betsy's keen affinity with gardeners everywhere trying to understand and discover the satisfaction of gardening outside the bounds of Anglo-European fashions and traditions. It happens that Betsy's particular fascination is with the genus *Salvia* and it is these that she ardently collects, grows and tries in new planting ideas. The book she has written on salvias seems a natural extension of her interest and her willingness to share her pleasure in them with others.

And what has this to do with the time to plant crocuses? It's easy really. There are many times when our plants fail to thrive, when seeds of new things will not germinate; when fresh design ideas do not flash across our minds eye with dazzling brightness; when carefully executed schemes don't work — in short, there are times when the whole idea of gardening in new directions becomes all too disspiriting. This disheartening time is the time when I plant crocuses, the wild crocuses of Greece and Turkey and Spain and Italy. Crocuses are what I plant when times of gardening change are hard to bear. Something to cheer me up. Something jewel-like, something to treasure, something that will remind me that hidden within my ideas the possibilities are there to create a garden that evolves and grows true to its own place. Take heed, though, that such times of gloominess may strike more than once. There is no shame in having several dozen pots of crocus that mark the struggle to achieve that goal. No shame either in having a dozen tubs of Oriental lilies for that matter if they serve to revive flagging energy for the task. I have at least that many myself and keep on making my garden in the sun and feel good about it too. What will you plant that will serve as a tonic? Just a little something in a pot that can be fussed over just a little as you go about the longer term task; something that will give your spirits a fillip but not divert you from the goal of creating a garden that has its own place under the sun.

seeds, sources & societies

SEEDS

USA

Bamert Seeds
Route 3, Box 1120
Muleshoe, Texas, 79347, USA

J L Hudson, Seedsman
PO Box 1058
Redwood City
California, 94064, USA

Larner Seeds
PO Box 407
235 Fern Road
Bolinas
California, 94924, USA

Native American Seed
3400 Long Prairie Road
Flower Mound
Texas, 75028, USA

S&S Seeds
PO Box 1275
Carpinteria
California, 93013, USA

Southwest Native Seeds
PO Box 50503
Tucson, Arizona, 85703, USA

Theodore Payne Foundation
10459 Tuxford Street
Sun Valley
California, 91352, USA

Thompson & Morgan
PO Box 1308
Farraday & Gramme Avenues
Jackson, NJ, 08527, USA

AUSTRALIA & NEW ZEALAND

Peter Dow & Co.
PO Box 696
Gisborne, 3800, New Zealand

New Zealand Tree Seeds
PO Box 435
Rangiora , 8254, New Zealand

Nindethana Seed Service
RMB 939
Woogenilup
West Australia, 6324, Australia

Southern Seeds
The Vicarage
Sheffield
Canterbury, New Zealand

SOUTH AFRICA

Silverhill Seeds
18 Silverhill Crescent
Kennilworth, 7700, Republic
of South Africa

UK & EUROPE

Jim & Jenny Archibald
Bryn Collen
Ffostrasol
Llandysul
Dyfed, SA44 5BS, Wales

Chiltern Seeds
Boretree Style
Ulverston
Cumbria , LA12 7PB, England

Jellito Seeds
Postfach 1264
D 29685
Schwarnstedt, Germany

John Morley
North Green Only
Stoven, Beccles
Suffolk
NR34 8DG, England

Dino Pelizzaro
290 chemin de Leouse
06220 Vallauris, France

Phedar Nursery (Will McLewin)
Bunkers Hill
Romiley
Stockport
SK6 3DS, England

CTDA Seeds (Dr Basil Smith)
174 Cambridge Street
London
SW1V 4QE, England

Richard Stockwell
64 Weardale Road
Sherwood
Nottingham
NG5 1DD, England

Thompson & Morgan
London Road
Ipswich
Suffolk
IP2 0BA, England

USA

Abbey Gardens
PO Box 2249
La Habra
California, 90632-2249, USA

A High Country Garden
2902 Rufina Street
Santa Fe
New Mexico, 87505-2929,
USA

Buena Creek Gardens
418 Buena Creek Road
San Marcos
California, 92069, USA

California Flora
PO Box 3
cnr Somers & D Street
Fulton
California, 95439, USA

Desert Moon Nursery
PO Box 600
Veguita
New Mexico, 87062, USA

Greenlee Nursery
301 East Franklin Avenue
Pomona
California, 91766, USA

Heirloom Roses
24062 NE Riverside Drive
St Paul
Oregon, 97137, USA

Hubbard Farms
PO Box 3446
Rancho Santa Fe
California, 92067, USA

Mesa Garden
PO Box 72
Belen
New Mexico, 87002, USA

Monterey Bay Nursery
748 San Miguel Canyon Road
PO Box 1296
Watsonville
California, 95077, USA

Mostly Natives
27235 Highway One
Box 258
Tomales
California, 94971, USA

New Mexico Cactus Research
PO Box 787
Belen
New Mexico, 87002, USA

**Jo O'Connell's Australian
Natives**
9040 North Ventura Avenue
Ventura
California, 93001, USA

Plants of the South West
Route 6, Box 11 – A
Santa Fe
New Mexico, 87501, USA

The Rose Ranch
PO Box 10087
Salinas
California, 93912-7087, USA

Sierra Azul Nursery
2660 East Lake Avenue
Watsonville
California, 95076, USA

**Tomlinson's Select Nurseries
(Palms and Cycads)**
3600 Bluebird Canyon Road
Vista
California, 92084, USA

**University of California, Santa
Cruz - Arboretum**
Santa Cruz
California, 95003, USA

Western Hills Nursery
16250 Coleman Valley Road
Occidental
California, 95465, USA

Yerba Buena Nursery
19500 Skyline Boulevard
Woodside
California, 94062, USA

Yucca Do Nursery
Peckerwood Gardens
PO Box 655
Waller
Texas, 77484, USA

AUSTRALIA & NEW ZEALAND

Aridaria Gardens
13 Alexander Avenue
RSD
Bilbaringa
South Australia, 5118,
Australia

Jocelyn Burnet
Andoran
Darkes Forest
New South Wales, 2058,
Australia

Ian Collier
PO Box 202
Civic Square
Canberra
Australian Capital Territory,
2608, Australia

The Diggers' Club
Heronswood
105 Latrobe Parade
Dromana
Victoria, 3936, Australia

Joy Plants (Terry Hatch)
Runciman Road R D 2
Pukekohe East
Auckland, New Zealand

**Kereru Nursery (Charlie
Challenger)**
Okuti Valley
Little River
Canterbury, New Zealand

Lambley Nursery (David Glenn)
Burnside
Lester's Road
Ascot
Victoria, 3364, Australia

**The Mail Box Gardeners (John
Wagner & John Mitchell)**
22 Excelsior Avenue
Castle Hill
New South Wales, 2154,
Australia

**Mathews Nursery (Lew & Kaye
Mathews)**
French Farm R D 2
Akaroa
Banks Peninsula, 8161, New
Zealand

**Melchester Nurseries
(Caudiciform succulents)**
PO Box 99
Kallangur
Queensland, 4503, Australia

Mildura Succulent Supplies
PO Box 756
Mildura
Victoria, 3502, Australia

Olive Tree Nursery
53 Green Street
Brompton
South Australia, 5007, Australia

Ron's Rare Palms and Cycads
c/o PO
Yandina
Queensland, 4561, Australia

Ross Roses
PO Box 23
Willunga
South Australia, 5172, Australia

Talisman Nursery
Ringawhati Road
Otaki, New Zealand

Terry's Garden Services (Cycads & Palms)
PO Box 78
Buddina
Queensland, 4575, Australia

Unlimited Perennials (Sue Templeton)
369 Boomerang Drive
Lavington
New South Wales, 2641, Australia

Jan Waddington's Nursery
RMB 1059
Kiewa Valley Highway
Kergunyah
Victoria, 3691, Australia

Woodbank Nursery (Ken Gillanders)
RMB 303
Kingston
Tasmania, 7150, Australia

UK & EUROPE

Arbor Exotica (Quercus sp.)
The Estate Office
Hall Farm
Weston Coleville
Cambridge, CB1 5PE, England

David Austin Roses
Bowling Green Lane
Albrighton
Wolverhampton, WV7 3HB, England

La Bambouseraie
Gènèrargues
30140, Langoudoc – Roussillon, France

Peter Beales
London Road
Attleborough
Norfolk, NR17 1AY, England

Beth Chatto's Nursery
White Barn House
Elmstead Market
Colchester
Essex, CO7 7DB, England

Bonout Elie
566 chemin des Maures
06600, Antibes, France

Cactées des Combes
04380 Thoard
Provence – Côte d'Azur, France

Fratelli Margheriti
loc. Monte S. Paolo
Chiusi (Siena), Italy

Iris en Provence
PB 53
83402 Hyères Cedex
Provence – Côte d'Azur, France

Jardins de Bel Air
Lieu dit Bel Air
Route de Campas
31620 Fronton
Midi – Pyrénées, France

Les Roses Anciennes
André Eve
Morailles
PB 206
Pithiviers-le-Vieil
45300 Pithiviers, France

Meilland Selections
Domaine de Saint André
La Camet-des-Maures
83340 Le Luc en Provence
Provence – Côte d'Azur, France

Pépinière Jean Rey
Domain de la Pascalette
83250 La Londe Les Maures
Provence – Côte d'Azur, France

Pépinière Filippi
Route Nationale 113
34140 Meze
Langoudoc – Roussillon, France

Pépinière Michèle Dental
1569 route de la Mer
06410
Binot/ Cannes, France

Pépinière de La Foux
chemin de La Foux
83220 Le Pradet, France

Vivai Guido Degl'Innocenti
Via Colle Ramole 7
loc. Bottai
50029 Tavarnuzze (Fl), Italy

Vivai Piante
Capitanio Stephano
Contrada Conchia 298
70043 Monopoli (Bari), Italy

Vivaio Corazza
C.P. 103
55045 Pietrasanta (L.U.), Italy

Texts on Sources
The Plant Finder – 40,000 plants and where to buy, C. Philip, pub. RHS, UK

20,000 plantes – Où et Comment les Acheter, F. et J. Cordier, La Maison Rustique, Paris

SOCIETIES

USA

Arizona Native Plant Society
PO Box 41206
Sun Station
Tucson
Arizona, 85717, USA

California Garden and Landscape History Society
c/o Barbara Barton
PO Box 1338
Sebastopol
California, 95473, USA

California Horticultural Society
California Academy of Sciences
Golden Gate Park
San Francisco
California, 94118, USA

California Native Plant Society
22 J Street, Suite 17
Sacramento
California, 95814, USA

Desert Demonstration Gardens
3700 W Charleston
Las Vegas

Nevada, 89153, USA

The International Centre for Earth Concerns
2162 Baldwin Road
Ojai
California, 93023, USA

International Oak Society
Secretary—M Nigel Wright
PO Box 310
Pen Argyl
Pennsylvania, 18072, USA

Native Plant Society of New
Mexico
    1302 Canyon Road
    Alamogordo
    New Mexico, 88310, USA

Native Plant Society of Texas
    P O Box 891
    Georgetown
    Texas, 78627, USA

The North American Rock
Garden Society
    Executive Secretary—Jacques
    Mommens
    PO Box 67
    Millwood
    New York, 10546, USA

Southern California
Horticultural Society
    PO Box 41080
    Los Angeles
    California, 90041, USA

Strybing Arboretum Society of
Golden Gate Park
    Ninth Avenue at Lincoln Way
    San Francisco
    California, 94122, USA

Utah Native Plant Society
    P O Box 520041
    Salt Lake City
    Utah, 84152, USA

Western Horticultural Society
    PO Box 60507
    Palo Alto
    California, 94306, USA

AUSTRALIA & NEW ZEALAND

The Australian Garden History
Society
    Membership Secretary
    c/o The Royal Botanic
    Gardens
    Birdwood Avenue
    South Yarra
    Victoria, 3141, Australia

The Society for Growing
Australian Plants
    c/o 17 Grandview Drive

Tea Tree Gully
South Australia, 5091, Australia

The New Zealand Alpine
Garden Society
    PO Box 2984
    Christchurch, New Zealand

SOUTH AFRICA

The Botanical Society of South
Africa
    c/o Kirstenbosch Botanical
    Garden
    Claremont, 7735, Republic of
    South Africa

UK & EUROPE

The Alpine Garden Society
    c/o The Secretary
    AGS Centre
    Avon Bank
    Pershore, Worcs., WR10 3JP,
    England

Amici dei Giardini Botanici
Hanbury
    Corso Montecarlo 13 bis
    18030 La Mortola (IM), Italy

Associacion Botanique de la
Vallée de la Garonne
    Mme Colette Soubrier
    La Présidente
    La Salicaire
    BP 14 bis
    82210 St Nicholas de la
    Grave, France

La Capelliana Garden Club
    Mr Tom Richfield
    Calle Segovia
    Urb. La Capelliana
    29630 Benalmadena, Malaga,
    Spain

Costa Blanca Gardeners' Circle
    Mrs Paula Hall
    La Casa Colmenar
    La Llosa de Camacho
    03759 Alicante, Spain

The Cyclamen Society
    c/o P J M Moore

Tile Barn House
Standen Street
Iden Green, Benenden
Kent, TN17 4LB, England

Mallorca (ESRA) Gardening
Club
    Mrs Ann Manning
    Font Xica
    Apartado 15
    Puerto Pollensa, 07470,
    Mallorca, Spain

Gesellschaft Der
Staudentfreunde
    c/o Mrs B Worfel
    Meisenweg 1
    65795, Hattersheim, Germany

The Hardy Plant Society
    c/o Mrs Dee Folkard
    67 Beaulieu Avenue
    Siddenham
    London, SE26 6TW, England

The Mediterranean Garden
Society
    PO Box 14
    Paenia 19002, Greece

The Royal Horticultural Society
    c/o The Membership
    Secretary
    80 Vincent Square
    London, SW1P 2PE, England

The Scottish Rock Garden Club
    c/o Miss K Gibb
    21 Merchiston Park
    Edinburgh, EH10 4PW,
    Scotland

Skiathos International Ladies
Gardening Club
    Mrs Norma Ashley-Smith
    Box 1
    37002 Skiathos, Greece

Société Nationale d'Horticulture
de France
    84 rue de Grenelle
    75007, Paris
    France

bibliography

Adams Robert & Marina, and Willens Alan
& Ann. *Dry Lands: Man and Plants*. The
Architectural Press, London, 1978.

Archer John, Hodges Jeffrey, LeHunt Bob.
The Water Efficient Garden. Random House, Sydney,
1993.

Ardiono H. *Catalogue des Plantes Vasculaires Qui Crossent
Spontanement aux Environs de Menton et de Monaco*.
Turin, 1862.

Barbour Michael, Pavlik Bruce, Drysdale Frank,
Lindstrom Susan. *California's Changing Landcapes*.
California Native Plant Society, Sacramento
(USA), 1993.

Bligh Beatrice. *Down to Earth*. Angus & Robertson,
Sydney, 1968.

Bowe Patrick. *Gardens of Portugal*. Tauris Parke, Paris,
1989.

Bradlow Frank R. *Francis Masson's "Account Of Three
Journey's At The Cape Of Good Hope"*, 1772–1775.
Tablecloth Press, Cape Town, 1994.

Brooke M, Kleinig D. *Field Guide To Eucalypts*.
(3 vols) Inkata, Sydney, 1994.

Brookes John. *Gardens of Paradise*. Weidenfeld
& Nicholson, London, 1989.

Cane Percy. *The Earth is my Canvas*. Methuen,
London, 1956.

Chatto Beth. *The Dry Garden*. J M Dent & Sons Ltd,
London, 1978.

Christopher Thomas. *Water-wise Gardening*. Simon &
Schuster, New York, 1994.

Church Thomas D. *Gardens are for People*. Reinhold,
New York, 1955.

Clebsch Betsy. *A Book of Salvias*. Timber Press,
Portland, (USA) 1997.

Clements Edith. *Flowers of Coast and Sierra*.
H W Wilson Co., New York, 1928.

Coate Barry. *Water Conserving Plants and Landscapes for
the Bay Area*. East Bay Municipal Utility District,
San Francisco, 1990.

Coffin David. *The Italian Garden*. Dumbarton Oaks,
Washington, 1972.

Cox Euan Hillhouse Methven (founder and editor).
New Flora and Silva. Dulau & Co. Ltd, London,
1929.

Cran Marion. *Gardens in America*. Macmillan, New
York, 1932.

Crowe Sylvia, Haywood Sheila. *The Gardens of
Mughal India*. Thames & Hudson, London, 1972.

Crowe Sylvia, Mitchell Mary. *The Pattern of Landscape*.
Packard, Chichester (UK), 1988.

De Mauny The Count. *The Gardens of Taprobane*.
Williams & Norgate Ltd., London, 1937.

Du Plessis Niel, Duncan Graham. *Bulbous Plants of
South Africa*. Tafelberg Publishers, Cape Town,
1989.

Du Cane Florence. *The Flowers and Gardens of Madeira*.
A & C Black, London, 1909.

Eckbo Garrett. *Landscapes for Living*. F W Dodge
Corp., New York, 1950.

Eggar Mrs H C. *An Indian Garden*. Murray, London,
1904.

Eliovsen Sima. *Flowering Trees and Shrubs for South
African Gardens*. The Standard Press, Cape Town,
1951.

Evans Ronald. *Handbook of Cultivated Sedums*. Science
Reviews Ltd., Northwood (UK), 1985.

Fagan Gwen. *Roses at the Cape of Good Hope*. Breestraat
Publikasies, Cape Town, 1988.

Fairchild David. *Exploring for Plants*. Macmillan, New
York, 1930.

Fink Augusta. *Monterey County*. Western Tanager
Press, Santa Cruz (USA) 1972.

Flannery Tim. *the future eaters*. Reed, Melbourne, 1994.

Francis Mark, Hester Randolf Jnr. *The Meaning of
Gardens*. MIT Press, Cambridge (USA), 1990.

French Jere Stuart. *The California Garden*. Landscape
Architecture Foundation, Washington, 1993.

Fullerton Alice. *To Persia for Flowers*. Oxford
University Press, London, 1938.

Galotti Jean. *Le Jardin et la Maison Arabes au Maroc*.
Editions Albert Levy, Paris, 1926.

Gardner Theodore Roosevelt (III). *Lotusland*. Allen Knoll Pub., Santa Barbara (USA), 1995.

Garnett Tommy. *Man of Roses: Alister Clark of Glenara*. Kangaroo Press, Sydney, 1990.

Gentry Howard Scott. *Agaves of Continental North America*. University of Arizona Press, Tucson (USA), 1982.

Gibbon Euell. *Stalking the Wild Asparagus*. McKay, New York, 1962.

Giddy Cynthia. *Cycads of South Africa*. Purnell, Cape Town, 1974.

Gildemeister Heidi. *Mediterranean Gardening: a Waterwise Approach*. Editorial Moll, Palma deMallorca, Spain, 1995.

Gilmer Maureen. *California Wildfire Landscaping*. Taylor Pub. Co., Dallas (USA) 1995.

Green Wilson Carol. *Alice Eastwood's Wonderland*. California Academy of Sciences, San Francisco, 1955.

Greenlee John. *The Encyclopedia of Ornamental Grasses*. Rodale Press, Emmaus (USA), 1992.

Hanbury Sir Cecil. *La Mortola Gardens*. Printed for private distribution by Oxford University Press, 1938.

Harbison Robert. *Eccentric Spaces*. Secker & Warburg, London, 1989.

Hartshorne Heather. *Plants for Dry Gardens*. Allen & Unwin, Sydney, 1995.

Hertrich William. *The Huntington Botanical Gardens*. The Huntington Library, San Marino (USA), 1949.

Hooker J D, Ball John. *Marocco and the Great Atlas*. Macmillan & Co., London, 1878.

Howard Sir Albert. *An Agricultural Testament*. Oxford University Press, London, 1940. (8th ed. Rodale Press, Emmaus (USA), 1979.)

Hunt James Fox, Wolschke-Bulmahn Joachim, eds. *The Vernacular Garden*. Dumbarton Oaks, Washington 1993.

Innes Clive. *The World of Iridaceae*. Holly Gate International, Ashington (UK), 1985.

Isaacs Jennifer. *Quirky Gardens*. University of Queensland Press, St Lucia (Australia) 1995.

Jacobsen Herman. *Lexicon of Succulent Plants*. Blandford, London, 1974.

Jarman Derek. *Derek Jarman's Garden*. Thames and Hudson, London, 1995.

Jellicoe Geoffrey & Susan. *The Landscape of Man*. Thames & Hudson, London, 1975.

Jensen Jens. *Siftings*. Johns Hopkins University Press, Baltimore, 1990.

Johnson Paul, Krell Dorothy. *The California Missions*. Sunset Pub., Menlo Park (USA) 1979.

Jones David L. *Palms Throughout The World*. Reed, Sydney, 1995.

Jones Louisa. *Gardens of the Riviera*. Flammarion, Paris, 1994.

Jones Louisa. *Gardens in Provence*. Flammarion, Paris, 1992.

Jones David L. *Cycads of the World*. Reed, Sydney, 1993.

Kelly Stan. *Eucalypts*. (Vols 1 and 2) Viking/Penguin, Melbourne, 1989.

King Ronald. *Tresco, England's Island of Flowers*. Constable, London, 1985.

Latymer Hugo. *The Mediterranean Gardener*. Francis Lincoln, London, 1990.

Lawson William. *A New Orchard and Garden*. Printed at London by Bar: Alsop for Roger Jackson and are to be sold at his shop neere Fleet-street Conduit, (3rd ed.) 1626. (My copy in facsimile by The Cresset Press Ltd, London, 1927.)

Lazzaro Claudia. *The Italian Renaissance Garden*. Yale University Press, New Haven, 1990.

Lighton Conrad. *Cape Floral Kingdom*. Juta & Co., Cape Town, 1961.

MacDougal Elisabeth, Ettinghausen Richard. *The Islamic Garden*. Dumbarton Oaks, Washington (USA), 1976.

MacDougal Elisabeth, Jashemski Wilhelmina. *Ancient Roman Gardens*. Dumbarton Oaks, Washington (USA), 1981.

Mallitz Jerome. *Personal Landscapes*. Timber Press, Portland (USA), 1989.

Maloney Betty. *All About Australian Bush Gardens*. Mulavon, Sydney, 1973.

Marret Leon. *Les Fleurs de la Côte D'Azur*. Paul Lechevalier, Paris, 1926.

Martineau Mrs Phillip. *Gardening in Sunny Lands*. Richard Cobden-Sanderson, London, 1924.

Masson Georgina. *Italian Gardens*. Thames & Hudson, London, 1961.

McVaugh Rogers. *Edward Palmer, Plant Explorer*. Norman, University of Oklahoma, 1956.

Menjili, de Corny- Irene. *Jardins du Maroc*. Le temps Apprivoises, Paris, 1991.

Menzies Yves. *Mediterranean Gardening*. John Murray, London, 1971.

Metcalf Lawrie. *The Cultivation of New Zealand Plants*. Godwit, Auckland, 1993.

Mielke Judy. *Native Plants for Southwestern Gardens*. University of Texas Press, Austin (USA), 1993.

Moore Charles, Mitchell William, Turnbull William Jnr. *The Poetics of Gardens*. MIT Press, Cambridge (USA), 1988.

More Than a Catalogue. Department of Primary Industries/State – Flora, Adelaide (Australia) 1992.

Morgenthau Fox Helen. *Patio Gardens*. Macmillan, New York, 1929.

Newton Wilbur Donald. *Persian Gardens and Garden Pavilions*. Dumbarton Oaks, Washington (USA), 1979.

Noailles Vicomte de, Lancaster Roy. *Mediterranean Plants and Gardens*. Floraisse, Paris, 1974.

Owen Jesse. *Mediterranean Gardening in Mallorca*. Alqueria Blance, Spain, undated.

Padilla Victoria. *Southern California Gardens*. University of California, Berkeley, 1961.

Panich Paula, Burba Trulsson Nora. *Desert Southwest Gardens*. Bantam, New York, 1990.

Pavlik Bruce, Muick Pamela, Johnson Sharon, Popper Marjorie. *Oaks of California*. Cachuma Press, Los Olivos (USA), 1992.

Perry Bob. *Landscape Plants for Western Regions*. Land Design Pub., Claremont (USA), 1992.

Perry Bob. *Trees and Shrubs for Dry California Landscapes*. Land Design Pub., San Dimas (USA), 1987.

Phillips Roger, Rix Martyn. *Perennials*. (2 vols) Pan Books, London, 1991.

Pinkva Donald, Gentry Howard Scott. *Symposium on the Genus Agave*. Special Issue of Desert Plants Vol. 7, No. 2, 1985.

Pitt Marcelle. *Gardening in Spain*. Lookout Pub., Spain, undated.

Polunin Olga, Huxley Anthony. *Flowers of the Mediterranean*. Chatto & Windus, London, 1979.

Power Goslee Nancy. *The Gardens of California*. Clarkson Potter, New York, 1995.

Quest-Ritson Charles. *The English Garden Abroad*. Viking, London, 1992.

Raunkiaer C. *The Life Forms of Plants*. Oxford (at the Clarendon Press) 1934.

Reynolds Gilbert W. *The Aloes of South Africa*. Aloes of South Africa Book Fund, Cape Town, 1970.

Rigby Geoff & Bev. *Colour Your Garden with Australian Natives*. Kangaroo Press, Sydney, 1992.

Rowntree Lester. *Flowering Shrubs of California*. Stanford University Press, Stanford (USA), 1947.

Rowntree Lester. *Hardy Californians*. Macmillan, New York, 1936.

Ruffinie're du Prey Pierre de la. *The Villas of Pliny*. University of Chicago, Chicago (USA), 1994.

Russell Vivian. *Gardens of the Riviera*. Little Brown, London, 1993.

Sackville-West Victoria. *Passenger to Tehran*. Hogarth Press, London, 1926. (2nd ed. Cockbird Press, Heathfield, UK, 1990.)

Saunders Charles Francis. *The Wild Gardens of Old California*. Wallace Herberd, Santa Barbara (USA) 1927.

Seddon George. *Sense of Place*. University of West Australia Press, Perth, 1972.

Smithers Sir Peter. *The Adventures of a Gardener*. RHS/Antique Collectors Club, London, 1995.

Standish Nichols Rose. *Italian Leisure Gardens*. Williams & Norgate, London, 1929.

Standish Nichols Rose. *Spanish and Portugese Gardens*. Houghton Miffin Co., Boston, 1924.

Starr-Dobyns Winifred. *California Gardens*. Macmillan, New York, 1931.

Stauffacher Solomon Barbara. *Green Architecture and the Green Revolution*. Rizzoli, New York, 1988.

Steele Fletcher. *Gardens and People*. Houghton Mifflin Co., Boston, 1964.

Stout Mary, Agar Mary. *A Book of Gardening for the Sub-Tropics*. H F & G Witherby, London, 1921.

Sumner Angier Belle. *The Garden Book of California*. Paul Elder & Co., San Francisco, 1906.

Tame Terry. *Acacias of Southeast Australia*. Kangaroo Press, Sydney, 1992.

Thompson H Stuart. *Flowering Plants of the Riviera*. Longmans Green, London, 1914.

Tunnard Christopher. *Gardens in the Modern Landscape*. The Architectural Press, London, 1948.

Turner Roger. *Euphorbias: a Gardener's Guide*. Batsford, London, 1995.

Underwood Mrs Desmond. *Grey and Silver Plants*. Collins, London, 1971.

Unknown author. *Wild Flowers of South Africa*. Struik Pub., Cape Town, 1980.

Unknown author. *The Amateur Gardener in the Hills*. Thacker, Spink & Co., Calcutta, 1881.

Van-Ollenbach Aubrey. *Planting Guide to the Middle East*. The Archtectural Press, London, 1978.

Villiers Stuart Constance. *Gardens of the Great Mughals*. A & C Black, London, 1913.

Walters James, Backhaus Balbir. *Shade and Colour with Water Conserving Plants*. Timber Press, Portland (USA) 1992.

Walther Eric. *Echeveria*. California Academy of Science, San Francisco, 1972.

Webber John Milton. *Yuccas of the Southwest*. US Department of Agriculture, Washington, 1953.

Wharton Edith. *Italian Villas and their Gardens*. The Century Co., New York, 1904.

White Mary E. *After the Greening: the Browning of Australia*. Kangaroo Press, Sydney, 1994.

Wrigley John, Fagg Murray. *Banksias, Waratahs & Grevilleas*. Angus & Robertson, Sydney, 1992.

Wrigley John, Fagg Murray. *Australian Native Plants*. William Collins, Sydney, 1980.

Wrigley John, Fagg Murray. *Bottlebrushes, Paperbarks & Teatrees*. Angus & Robertson, Sydney, 1995.

index